Warship Recognition Guide 2024

ISBN: 979-8-321645-52-9 (Paperback)
ISBN: 979-8-321646-14-4 (Hardcover)

The views expressed in this publication are those of the author and do not necessarily reflect the official policy or position of the Department of Defense or the U.S. government. The public release clearance of this publication by the Department of Defense does not imply Department of Defense endorsement or actual accuracy of the material.

The content of this book is for informational purposes only and is not intended as a source of analysis, definitive or exhaustive inventory, or description of the listed warship classes. You understand that the purpose of this publication is to facilitate warship recognition and as a source of valuable information for the reader.

Although the publisher and the author have made every effort to ensure that the information in this publication was correct at press time and while this publication is designed to provide accurate information in regard to the subject matter covered, the publisher and the author assume no responsibility for errors, inaccuracies, omissions, or any other inconsistencies herein and hereby disclaim any liability to any party for any loss, damage, or disruption caused by errors or omissions, whether such errors or omissions result from negligence, accident, or any other cause.

Front cover image compiled from U.S. Navy, Israel Defense Forces, and Ministry of Defense of Russia photographs.

Printed in the United States of America.

Third printed edition. 2024.

TABLE OF CONTENTS

FOREWORD

The world is in an era of great power competition – and the maritime domain is the primary, global theater. The United States of America, the People's Republic of China, and the Russian Federation stand in competition across the globe. As more than 90 percent of the world's trade by volume travels by water, the world's oceans are critical highways and a source of security challenges. All three competitors deploy large navies to protect free navigation of the seas and further their national interests. This book assists the sailor, student, and the layman in recognizing the warships of these countries.

America

The world's preeminent maritime power, the United States of America has relied heavily on shipping and freed navigation of the sea since its founding. Blessed with extensive coastlines on both the Atlantic and Pacific Oceans, America has maintained the world's most powerful navy since World War II. However, the United States Navy (USN) is facing challenges stemming from global commitments and a shrinking, aging fleet. Caught between renewed government interest in increasing the size of the Navy, the long lead-time necessary for warship production, and the onset of retirements of Cold War-era vessels, the USN continues to shrink. The 2023 President's budget saw plans for extensive retirements of aging vessels without immediate replacement, including aging *Ticonderoga*-class guided missile cruisers and *Cyclone*-class patrol ships as well as the much newer *Freedom*-class littoral combat ships. Current projections estimate that the USN's battle fleet will number 290 by 2030 do not compare favorably with China's anticipated growth to 435. While delays inhibit production of the *Constellation* guided missile frigate class and the *Columbia* nuclear-powered ballistic missile submarine class, production of the *Arleigh Burke*-class Flight III guided missile destroyers and *Virginia*-class nuclear-powered attack submarine ensure that America retains significant sea power.

China

China continues to rise as a sea power. While underway for three decades, China's modernization and expansion of its fleet continues to drive consternation about its intentions and burgeoning capability. US officials anticipate that the People's Liberation Army Navy (PLAN) will grow to 395 warships by 2025 and 435 by 2030. China's acquisition of three aircraft carriers – and production of an additional carrier – indicate Beijing's interest in blue-water operations and power projection abroad. Coupled with joint Chinese-Russian patrols in the Pacific, China is demonstrating growing confidence in its naval operations and capabilities. China's continued acquisition of *Renhai* class guided missile cruiser, *Luyang III*-class guided missile destroyer, *Shang* nuclear-powered attack submarine class, and *Yuan* diesel electric submarine class expand both China's fleet size and capabilities at sea. Continued production of the *Yushen* amphibious assault ship class and *Yuzhao* amphibious ship class further augment the PLAN's ability to support amphibious operations, such as in the vicinity of Taiwan or China's disputed claims in the South China Sea. China's growing strength at sea enable military options to advance its interests worldwide.

Russia

Russia's navy continues to modernize despite the ongoing and primarily ground-conflict occurring in Ukraine. Beyond the 2022 loss of the Russian Black Sea Fleet's Slava-class guided missile cruiser *Moskva*, Russia has taken losses to its amphibious transport vessels, reducing its logistical capacity in the Black Sea. Increased attacks by Ukrainian cruise missiles and unmanned surface vessels (USVs) have pushed Russia to move its Black Sea vessels from Sevastopol in Crimea to its base at Novorossiysk in the northern Caucasus. Even so, Russia warships continue to harm Ukraine's economy by restricting Ukraine's ability to export by sea, launch Kalibr missiles into Ukraine, and maintain sea control over much of the northern Black Sea. Russia continues to modernize its aging Soviet-legacy cruisers and destroyers while launching new (and smaller) Kalibr-missile capable frigates and corvettes. Likewise, Russia's submarine fleet received new *Borei*-class nuclear-powered ballistic missile submarines, *Severodvinsk*-class nuclear-powered cruise missile submarines, and both *Kilo* and *Lada*-class disel-electric attack submarines and retired its last *Typhoon*-class nuclear-powered ballistic missile submarine in February 2023, ending the service of the world's largest submarines ever built. Russia's navy is a green-water one, despite its blue-water navy aspirations captured in its 2022 Maritime Doctrine. In addition to its Black Sea operations, and joint patrols with China in the Pacific, continued Russian activity in the eastern Mediterranean and the Arctic demonstrate Russia's capacity for global presence even while fielding a green-water navy with limited power projection capability.

ABOUT

This recognition guide focuses on identification of 107 ship classes by their most prominent physical characteristics: hulls, masts, radar aerials, funnels, and major weapons systems. This guide also provides information on embarked aviation, both manned and unmanned. Where available, each ship class includes its indigenous and NATO names. Each entry has been categorized into nine warship types:

- Aircraft Carriers
- Amphibious Ships
- Cruisers
- Destroyers
- Frigates
- Corvettes
- Mine Warfare Ships
- Patrol Ships
- Submarines

Each section is presented in alphabetical order; first by country, then by class name, without regard to a ship's strategic, operational, or tactical importance. National orders of battle constantly change with ship retirements, shipyard maintenance, sales to other countries, and acquisitions of new classes and constructions. This guide includes details of 107 classes and provides the names and pennant numbers of the ships in each class, where available.

Aircraft Carriers

Gerald R. Ford

Class: Gerald R. Ford (CVN)

US Navy Photo

Country of Origin: United States of America

Operators: United States of America

Active: 1 + 1 in trials

Building: 2

Name (Pennant Number): GERALD R. FORD (78), JOHN F. KENNEDY (79), ENTERPRISE (80), DORIS MILLER (81)

SPECIFICATION
Displacement, tons: 100,000.

Length, feet (meters): 1040 (317) wl.

Beam, feet (meters): 134 (40.8) wl.

Draft, feet (meters): 39 (11.9).

Flight deck length, feet (meters): 1092 (332.8) oa.

Flight deck width, feet (meters): 256 (78) oa.

Speed, knots: 30+.

Complement: 4,539. (508 Officers, 3,789 Enlisted).

ARMAMENT
Missiles: SSM – 2 x 8 (16) Mk 29 GMLS with RIM-162 ESSM, SAM – 2 x 21 (42) Mk 49 GMLS with RIM-116 RAM.

Guns: 3 x Mk 15 Phalanx CIWS.

Electronic: AN/SLQ-32.

Decoys: Mk 53 Nulka decoy launch system.

SENSORS
Air search: AN/SPY-3 AESA; AN/SPY-4 VSR (78-only)

Air/Surface search: AN/SPY-6 AMDR (79 and up)

RECOGNITION FEATURES

- Flat flight deck.
- Large island aft of midships.
- Isolated mast fore of midships.
- Dual, horizontal funnel built into starboard-side sponson before midships.
- Aerial radars mounted on all sides of island.
- Radome mounted on starboard-side sponson protruding after of island.
- Phalanx CIWS located on sponsons starboard-side before midships, port-side midships, and starboard stern.
- Octuple SAM missile launch boxes on sponsons starboard-side before midships and port stern.
- RAM mountings on sponsons port-side before midships and starboard stern.

Navigation: AN/SPY-3 AESA, AN/SPY-6 AMDR

Fire control: AN/SPY-3, AN/SPY-6 AMDR

AIR SUPPORT
Equipped with EMALS replacement of traditional CATOBAR system

Fixed-wing aircraft: 75-90 in carrier air wing, including F/A-18E-Super Hornet; F-35C Lightning II, E-2C Hawkeye, EA-16G Growler, and MV-22B Osprey.

Helicopters: MH-60R Seahawk; MH-60S Seahawk.

Nimitz

Class: Nimitz (CVN)

Country of Origin: United States of America

Operators: United States of America

Active: 10

Name (Pennant Number): NIMITZ (68), DWIGHT D EISENHOWER (69), CARL VINSON (70), THEODORE ROOSEVELT (71), ABRAHAM LINCOLN (72), GEORGE WASHINGTON (73), JOHN C STENNIS (74), HARRY S TRUMAN (75), RONALD REAGAN (76), GEORGE H W BUSH (77)

SPECIFICATION

Displacement, tons: 97,000.

Length, feet (meters): 1040 (317) wl.

Beam, feet (meters): 134 (40.8) wl.

Draft, feet (meters): 40 (12.2).

Flight deck length, feet (meters): 1092 (332.8) oa.

Flight deck width, feet (meters): 252 (76.8) oa.

Speed, knots: 30+.

Complement: 5,000-5,200 (3,000-3,200 Ship's Company, 1,500 Air Wing, 500 Other).

ARMAMENT

Missiles: SAM – 2-3 x RIM-7 Sea Sparrow, 3-4 RIM-116 RAM.

Guns: 3-4 x Mk 15 Phalanx CIWS.

Electronic: AN/SLQ-32A(V)4.

Decoys: 4 Mk 36 SRBOC launchers; SLQ-25A torpedo decoy.

US Navy Photo

RECOGNITION FEATURES

- Elongated rectangular island on starboard-side aft of midships.
- Square radar aerial atop forward end of island, above bridge.
- Complex pole mainmast atop central bridge with multiple aerials.
- Enclosed isolated mast aft of island supports curved lattice radar aerial.
- Radome mounted on port-side sponson, forward CIWS/RAM.
- 2 CIWS/RAM mountings fitted 1 port, and 1 starboard below flight deck overhang.
- Octuple SAM missile launchers mounted on port side at flight deck narrowing, and on sponsons port and starboard.

SENSORS

Air search: AN/SPS-48E, AN/SPS-49(V)5.

Surface search: SPS-67(V)1.

Navigation: SPS-65(V)9.

Traffic control: AN/SPN-41, AN/SPN-43C, A/N-46.

Fire control: Mk 91 (NSSM), Mk 95.

AIR SUPPORT

Fixed-wing aircraft: Approximately 60 in carrier air wing, including 48 x F/A-18E-F Super Hornet, 4 x E-2C Hawkeye, 4 x EA-16G Growler, CVM-22B Osprey.

Helicopters: 4 x MH-60R Seahawk, 2 x MH-60S Seahawk.

Admiral Kuznetsov

Class: Admiral Kuznetsov (CV)

Country of Origin: Soviet Union

Operators: China, Russia

Active: 2 (1 China, 1 Russia) + 1 in sea trials (China)
Name (Pennant Number): ADMIRAL
KUZNETSOV, LIAONING (16), SHANDONG
(17)

SPECIFICATION
Displacement, tons: 58,000, 70,000

(Shandong)*.

Length, feet (meters): 886 (270), wl.

Beam, feet (meters): 114'10" (35) wl.

Draft, feet (meters): 32'10" (10).

Flight deck length, feet (meters): 1,001 (305),

1,033 (315)* oa.

Flight deck width, feet (meters): 236'3" (72),

246 (75)* oa.

Speed, knots: 30.

Range, miles: 3,850 at 29 kts, 8,500 at 18 kts.

Complement: 2,356; 2,626*.

ARMAMENT
Missiles: SSM – 12 x Chelomey SS-N-19

Shipwreck (Granit) launchers. SAM – 4 x Altair

SA-N-9 Gauntlet (Klinok) sextuple vertical

launchers, 8 x SA-N-11 Grisson. 3 x HQ-10

(China) CIWS

Guns: 8 x Altair CADS-N-1 Kortik/Kashtan

twin 30 mm CIWS. 3 x H/PJ12 (China).

Electronic: ECM suite

Depth charges: 2 x RBU 12000 (Russia).

Decoys: 19 x PK 10, 4 x PL 2 chaff launchers

(Russia) 4 x 24 launcher tubes; 2 x 16 launcher

tubes (China).

SENSORS
Air search: Sky Watch 3D; Type 346 Dragon

Eye (China).

Ministry of Defense of Japan Photo

Traffic Control: Fly Trap B.

Surface search: Strut Pair.

Navigation: Palm Frond.

Fire control: Cross Sword (SAM), Hot Flash,

Type 347G Rice Bowl

Sonars: MGK-355 Polinom/Bull Horn hull-

mounted, LF VDS Platina /Horse Tail towed

array.

AIR SUPPORT
Fixed-wing aircraft: 18 Su-27K/Su-33 Flanker

D (air defense); 4 Su-25UTG Frogfoot

(attack/strike). 32 J-15.

Helicopters: 15; Ka-27PL Helix (ASW); 2 x Ka-

31 RLD Helix (AEW); 8 x Z-18 Super Frelon; 4

x Z-9 Haitun.

Fujian

Class: Fujian Type 003 (CV)

Country of Origin: China	
Operators: China	

Active: 1 in sea trials.

Name (Pennant Number): FUJIAN (018).

SPECIFICATION
Displacement, tons: 85,000.

Length, feet (meters): 1,049'10" (320) oa, 984'4" (300) wl.

Beam, feet (meters): 249'4" (76) oa, 131'3" (40) wl.

Draft, feet (meters): 39'4" (12).

Flight deck length, feet (meters): 240 (73)

Speed, knots: 30+.

Complement: 3,000 Ship's Company, 2,500 Air Wing.

ARMAMENT
Missiles: SAM – 2-4 x HQ-10.

Guns: 2-4 x H/PJ12 CIWS.

Decoys: 4 x 24 launcher tubes; 2 x 16 launcher tubes.

SENSORS
Air search: Type 346B Dragon Eye, X-band radar.

Ministry of National Defense of China Photo

RECOGNITION FEATURES
- Elongated flat-deck with overhang forward of hull, running to stern.
- Single, rectangular pyramid island fitted starboard-side amidships.
- Weapons mounts on sponsons fitted port and starboard of flight deck, forward of midships.
- Two weapons mounts fitted on sponsons at port-side and starboard-side stern.
- Two aircraft elevators fitted forward and aft of starboard-side island.
- Hexagonal enclosed mast fitted atop island.
- Exhaust vents incorporated into single island.

Note: Fujian is equipped with EMALS CATOBAR system.

Surface search: Type 360S Seagull air-surface.

Navigation: Type 360S Seagull air-surface.

AIR SUPPORT
Fixed-wing aircraft: approximately 40, including 24-26 x J-15, J-35 fighters; JZY-01, KJ-600 air early warning and control.

Helicopters: Z-20.

America

Class: America (LHA)

US Navy Photo

Country of Origin: America	
Operators: America	
Active: 2	
Building: 2	
Planned: 11	

Name (Pennant Number): AMERICA (6), TRIPOLI (7), BOUGAINVILLE (8), FALLUJAH (9).

SPECIFICATION
Displacement, tons: 45,700.

Length, feet (meters): 844 (257) wl.

Beam, feet (meters): 106 (32) wl.

Draft, feet (meters): 26 (7.9).

Speed, knots: 22+.

Complement: 1,059 (65 Officers, 994 Enlisted) + 1,687 Troops.

ARMAMENT
Missiles: SAM – 2 x RIM-162 ESSM, 2 x RIM-116 RAM.

Guns: 2 x Phalanx CIWS; 3 x Mk 38 25mm MG.

Electronic: AN/SLQ-32B(V)2 EW suite

Decoys: 2 x Mk-53 Nulka.

SENSORS
Long Range Air Search: AN/SPS-49(V)5 2D.

Air search: AN/SPS-48 3D.

RECOGNITION FEATURES
- Continuous, flat flight deck.
- 2 distinctive starboard-slanted funnels built into starboard, rectangular mast.
- Rectangular mast mounted starboard, aft of midships.
- Extended bridge mounted forward of rectangular mast.
- RIM-116 RAM launcher and octuple quad ESSM launcher placed forward of mast.
- CIWS mounted starboard-side stern.
- RAM missile launcher mounted port stern.
- Large, rectangular radar dish mounted port of first funnel above rectangular mast.

Traffic control: AN/SPN-43C.

Surface search: AN/SPQ-9B.

Navigation: SPS-65(V)9.

Fire control: AN/SPQ-9B.

AIR SUPPORT
Fixed-wing aircraft:: 10 x AV-8B Harrier or F-35B Lightning II VSTOL.

Helicopters: 8 x AH-1W/Z Super Cobra/Viper (Attack); 12 x MV-22B Osprey; 4 x CH-53E Super Stallion; 4 x MH-60 Seahawk.

Wasp

US Navy Photo

Class: Wasp (LHD)

Country of Origin: America	
Operators: America	

Active: 7

Name (Pennant Number): WASP (1), ESSEX (2), KEARSARGE (3) BOXER (4), BATAAN (5), IWO JIMA (7), MAKIN ISLAND (8)

SPECIFICATION

Displacement, tons: 40,532.

Length, feet (meters): 819 (249.6) wl.

Beam, feet (meters): 104 (31.8) wl.

Draft, feet (meters): 27 (8.1).

Flight deck length, feet (meters): 843 (257)oa.

Flight deck width, feet (meters): 140 (42.6)oa.

Speed, knots: 22.

Range, miles: 9,500 at 18 kts.

Complement: 1,070 (66 Officers, 1,004 Enlisted).

ARMAMENT

Missiles: SAM –2 x RIM-7 Sea Sparrow launchers. 2 x RIM-116 RAM.

Guns: 3 x 20 mm Phalanx Mk 15 CIWS, 3 x 25 mm Mk 38 chain guns; 4 x .50cal/12.7mm MG.

Decoys: 1 x SRBOC 6-barrel Mk 36; SLQ-25 Nixie torpedo decoy; SLQ-49 chaff buoys.

SENSORS

Air search: AN/SPS-48 3D, AN/SPS-49(V)7 2D; Mk 23 TAS.

Air Traffic: AN/SPN-35, AN/URN-25 TACAN.

Surface search: SPS-67, AN/SYS-2(V)1.

Navigation: SPS-64(V)9.

RECOGNITION FEATURES

- Continuous flat flight deck.
- Elongated starboard island amidships.
- CIWS mounted atop bridge, and at starboard-side stern. (!-4) have additional CIWS at port-side stern.
- Mk 29 launchers mounted forward bridge and center at stern. Mk 49 RAM mounted forward of bridge Mk 29 launcher and port-side stern.
- 2 black-tipped funnels, fore and aft atop island.
- 2 pole masts atop island; taller mast is aft.
- 2 aircraft elevators, 1 starboard and aft of island, 1 port midships.
- Floodable stern door with well deck supports amphibious assault capability.

Fire control: Mk 91.

AIR SUPPORT

Fixed-wing aircraft:: 6-20 x AV-8B Harrier or F-35B Lightning II (VSTOL).

Helicopters: 4 x AH-1W/Z Super Cobra/Viper (Attack); 12-22 x MV-22B Osprey; 4 x CH-53E Super Stallion; 3-4 x UH-1Y Venom.

CAPACITY

Troops: 1,687.

Vehicles: 40 armored amphibious vehicles or 3 LCAC or 2 LCU.

Yushen

Class: Yushen Type 075 (LHD)

Xinghai Military Image (CC BY 4.0)

Country of Origin: China	
Operators: China	

Active: 3

Building: 1

Name (Pennant Number): HAINAN (31), GUANGXI (32), ANHUI (33).

SPECIFICATION
Displacement, tons: 40,000.

Length, feet (meters): 777'7" (237) wl.

Beam, feet (meters): 98'5" (30) wl.

Draft, feet (meters): 27'11" (8.5).

Flight deck length, feet (meters): 820'3" (250) oa.

Flight deck width, feet (meters): 118'1" (36) oa.

Speed, knots: 25.

Complement: 1,100.

ARMAMENT
Missiles: SAM – 2 x 24 (48) HHQ-10.

Guns: 2 x H/PJ-11 30mm CIWS.

Electronic: ECM suite.

Decoys: 4 x 24 (48) launcher tubes; 2 x 16 (32) launcher tubes.

RECOGNITION FEATURES
- Flat, continuous flight deck.
- Dual islands atop starboard superstructure amidships.
- H/PJ-11 CIWS mounted on sponsons port-side forward of midships and starboard-side stern.
- HHQ-10 SAM launchers mounted on sponsons before the bridge superstructure and port-side stern.
- Decoy launchers mounted on four sponsons located two starboard-side and two port-side before and aft of midships.

SENSORS
Air search: H/LJQ-382 3D long-range.

Air Traffic: Type 754A (helicopter).

Fire control: Type 347G Rice Bowl.

AIR SUPPORT
Helicopters: 30; Z-8CJ Super Frelon, Z-18F Super Frelon (ASW); Z-18J Super Frelon (ASW); Z-9 Haitun.

CAPACITY
Cargo, tons: 1,000.

Troops: 1,600.

Vehicles: 35 armored amphibious vehicles and 3 x Type 726 LCAC.

Ivan Rogov

LeAZ-1977 Photo (CC BY 4.0)

Class: Ivan Rogov Project 23900 (LHD)

Country of Origin: Russia	
Operators: Russia	

Active: 0

Building: 2

Name (Pennant Number): IVAN ROGOV (---), MITROFAN MOSKALENKO (---).

SPECIFICATION

Displacement, tons: 30,000 standard, 40,000 full.

Length, feet (meters): 721'9" (220) oa.

Beam, feet (meters): 124'8" (38) oa.

Draft, feet (meters): 24'7" (7.5).

Speed, knots: 22.

Range, miles: 7,000 at 16 kts.

Complement: 320.

ARMAMENT

Missiles: SAM – 2 x 4 (8) for 9M311K Kortik/SA-N-11 Grison (CIWS).

Guns: 1 x 100mm A190 gun, 2 x 3M870-1F Pantsir-M CIWS, 3 x 30mm Kortik/CADS-N-1 Kashtan CIWS.

RECOGNITION FEATURES

- Flat flight deck.
- Sloped elongated hexagonal island at starboard, midships.
- Two enclosed masts atop island, forward mounted atop bridge roof and after mounted after
- Pozitiv aerial mounted atop forward mast atop bridge in island.
- 2 CIWS mounted port and starboard atop island, between forward and aft masts.
- 2 CIWS mounted forward midships port and starboard on sponsons outboard flight deck.

Note: Landing ships deploy from stern doors.

AIR SUPPORT

Helicopters: 16 x Ka-27 Helix/KA-29 (ASW) Helix-B/Ka-31 Helix/Ka-52K Alligator.

Unmanned Aerial Vehicles: 4 x S-70 Okhotnik-B.

CAPACITY

Cargo, tons: 1,000.

Troops: 900.

Vehicles: 75 armored vehicles, or 4 landing craft.

15

Amphibious Ships

Blue Ridge

Class: Blue Ridge (LCC)

US Navy Photo

Country of Origin: America	
Operators: America	

Active: 2

Name (Pennant Number): BLUE RIDGE (19), MOUNT WHITNEY (20).

SPECIFICATION
Displacement, tons: (19) 19,648, (20) 19,760.

Length, feet (meters): 636'6" (194) oa.

Beam, feet (meters): 108 (32.9) oa.

Draft, feet (meters): 289 (8.8).

Speed, knots: 23.

Range, miles: 13,000 at 16 kts.

Complement: 842 (52 Officers, 790 Enlisted).

ARMAMENT
Guns: 2 x Mk 15 Phalanx CIWS.

Decoys: 4 x Mk 36 SRBOC, AN/SLQ-25 Nixie

torpedo decoy.

SENSORS
Air search: AN/SPS-40B/C.

Surface search: AN/SPS-67.

Navigation: AN/SPS(59)V, SPS-64(V)9.

AIR SUPPORT
Helicopters: 1 x SH-60 Seahawk (ASW).

RECOGNITION FEATURES
- Level maindeck running from bow to stern, with distinctive flared hull midships.
- Square superstructure fitted midships with bridge extended out port and starboard.
- Tall, "T" shaped mast fitted atop superstructure, after bridge.
- Multiple aerials and masts fitted atop maindeck, including tall lattice mast mid-way between bows and superstructure.
- Multiple radar aerials mounted from bow to stern.
- Enclosed, pyramidal mast fitted atop maindeck, after of superstructure and forward of flight deck at stern.
- 1 CIWS mounted on forecastle, 1 mounted aft on sponson.

General Frank S. Besson Junior

Class: General Frank. S. Besson Jr. (LSV)

Country of Origin: America	
Operators: America	

Active: 8

Name (Pennant Number): GEN FRANK S BESSON JR (1), CW3 HAROLD C. CLINGER (2), GEN BREHON B SOMERVELL (3), LT GEN WILLIAM B BUNKER (4), MGEN CHARLES P GROSS (5), SP 4 JAMES A LOUX (6), SSGT ROBERT T. KURODA (7), MGEN ROBERT SMAILS (8).

SPECIFICATION

Displacement, tons: 1,612 light, 4,199 full.

Length, feet (meters): 83'2" (25.34) oa, (7-8) 95'5" (29.08) oa.

Beam, feet (meters): 18'2" (5.54) wl.

Draft, feet (meters): 3'8" (1.12), (7-8) 5'10' (1.76).

Speed, knots: 12.

RECOGNITION FEATURES

- Elevated forecastle with break in hull aft of forecastle to level maindeck
- Ire mast mounted on forecastle.
- Tall, "T" shaped mast fitted atop superstructure, after bridge.
- Two exhaust vents mounted atop bridge superstructure, port and starboard after bridge.

Range, miles: 5,500 at 12 kts,(7-8)5,500 at 8kts.

Complement: 30 (6 Officers, 24 Enlisted).

SENSORS

Navigation: Deca BridgeMaster-E ARPA (X-band, S-band).

Harpers Ferry

US Navy Photo

Class: Harpers Ferry (LSD)
Country of Origin: America

Operators: America

Active: 4
Name (Pennant Number): HARPERS
FERRY (49), CARTER HALL (50), OAK HILL
(51), PEARL HARBOR (52).

SPECIFICATION
Displacement, tons: 11,600 standard, 16,750
full.
Length, feet (meters): 609'6" (185.8) oa.
Beam, feet (meters): 84 (25.6) oa.
Draft, feet (meters): 20'6" (6.3).
Speed, knots: 22.
Range, miles: 8,000 at 18 kts.
Complement: 349 (22 Officers, 327 Enlisted).

ARMAMENT
Missiles: SAM – 2 x Mk 49 RAM.
Guns: 2 x Mk 15 Phalanx CIWS, 6 x .50-in
cal./12.7mm. MG, 2 x 25mm Mk 38 Bushmaster
gun.
Decoys: 6 x Mk 36 SRBOC, AN/SLQ-25 Nixie
torpedo decoy.

SENSORS
Air search: AN/SPS-49(V)5.
Surface search: AN/SPS-67V.
Navigation: AN/SPS-64(V)9.

AIR SUPPORT
Helicopters: 2 x SH-60B or MH-60R Seahawk.

CAPACITY
Troops: 500.
Vehicles: 2 LCAC or 1 LCU or 4 LCM-8 or 9
LCM-6 or 15 amphibious assault vehicle.

RECOGNITION FEATURES

- Level forecastle with forward wire mast at bow.
- Rectangular superstructure forward of midships, sheer to sides.
- Lattice mainmast supports radar aerials mid-superstructure.
- Aft-sloped funnel at aft end of superstructure.
- 2 CIWS mountings atop main superstructure, 1 forward of bridge, 1 immediately forward of funnel.
- RAM launchers atop bridge roof and at aft end of superstructure.
- 2 cranes mounted after funnel on extended quarterdeck.
- Flight deck supports helicopter operations, but no hangar onboard.

Note: Harpers Ferry-class LSD is very similar in appearance to Whidbey Island-class LSD. Harpers Ferry has CIWS forward of bridge, RAM launcher mounted atop bridge.

LCAC 1

Class: LCAC 1 (LCAC)

US Navy Photo

Country of Origin: America	
Operators: America	

Active: 81

Name (Pennant Number): 2, 4, 7, 8, 9, 10, 14, 15, 16,17, 19, 20, 21, 23, 24, 25, 26, 27, 28, 29, 30, 31, 32, 33, 34, 35, 36, 37, 38, 39, 40, 41, 42, 43, 44, 45, 46, 47, 48, 49, 50, 51, 52, 53, 54, 55, 56, 57, 58, 59, 60, 62, 63, 64, 65, 66, 67, 68, 69, 70, 71, 72, 73, 74, 75, 76, 77, 78, 79, 80, 81, 82, 83, 84, 85, 86, 87, 88, 89, 90, 91

RECOGNITION FEATURES

- Air cushion-inflated hovercraft.
- Two distinctive ring shrouds for air propellers mounted at stern, port and starboard.
- Bridge mounted forward, starboard side.
- Exhaust vents mounted forward of midships, after bridge.

Note: Bow opens for roll-on/roll-off loading capability.

SPECIFICATION

Displacement, tons: 93.4 light, 166.6 fl.

Length, feet (meters): 26'10" (8.17) oa.

Beam, feet (meters): 14'4" (4.37) oa.

Draft, feet (meters): 9" (0.24).

Speed, knots: 54, 40 when loaded.

Range, miles: 223 at 48 kts (light), 200 at 40 kts (loaded).

Complement: 5 + 24 troops/180 troops in personnel mode.

SENSORS

Navigation: Marconi CMR-91 Seemaster or Decca Bridge Master nav.

LCM 8

Class: LCM 8 (LCM)

Country of Origin: America	
Operators: America	

Active: 35

Name (Pennant Number):

SPECIFICATION

Displacement, tons: 34 light, 121 full

Length, feet (meters): 22'5" (6.84) oa.

Beam, feet (meters): 6'5" (1.96) oa.

Draft, feet (meters): 1'6" (0.45).

Speed, knots: 9.

Range, miles: 190 at 9 kts (loaded).

Complement: 5 Enlisted.

CAPACITY

Cargo, tons: 60.
Troops: 150.

RECOGNITION FEATURES

- Forward-slanted flat bow, opens to allow RO/RO loading and unloading.
- Open well-deck runs from bow to bridge superstructure at stern.
- Well-deck sides particularly wide, running smoothly from bow to stern.
- Bridge superstructure mounted at stern.
- Navigation radar mounted atop bridge.

LCU 1610

Class: LCU 1610 (LCU)

Country of Origin: America

Operators: America

Active: 32

Name (Pennant Number): 1616, 1617, 1619, 1627, 1629, 1630, 1631, 1632, 1633, 1634, 1635, 1643, 1644, 1645, 1646, 1648, 1649, 1650, 1651, 1653, 1654, 1655 1656, 1657, 1658, 1659, 1660, 1661, 1662, 1663, 1664, 1665, 1666, 1680, 1681.

RECOGNITION FEATURES

- Forward-slanted flat bow, opens to allow RO/RO loading and unloading.
- Open well-deck runs from bow to stern.
- Bridge mounted amidships, starboard-side.
- Enclosed, aft-angled mast mounted atop bridge.

SPECIFICATION

Displacement, tons: 170 light, 437 full, (1680-1681) 404 full.

Length, feet (meters): 41'1" (12.52) oa.

Beam, feet (meters): 9'1" (2.76) oa.

Draft, feet (meters): 2'1" (0.63).

Speed, knots: 11.

Range, miles: 1,200 at 11 kts.

Complement: 10 (10 Enlisted), (1680, 1681) 12 (2 Officers, 10 Enlisted).

ARMAMENT
Guns: 2 x 12.7mm MG.

SENSORS
Navigation: Furuno.

Lewis B. Puller

Class: Lewis B. Puller (ESB)

Country of Origin: America

Operators: America

Active: 4

Building: 2

Name (Pennant Number): LEWIS B. PULLER
(3), HERSHEL "WOODY" WILLIAMS (4),
MIGUEL KEITH (5), JOHN. L. CANLEY (6),
ROBERT E. SIMANEK (7), HECTOR A.
CAFFERATA JR. (8).

US Navy Photo

RECOGNITION FEATURES

- Distinctive, elevated forecastle with significant break in hull aft forecastle to level maindeck.
- Distinctive flight deck raised from midships, running between forward and aft (bridge) superstructures.
- Tripod mast atop forward superstructure.
- Dual, black-tipped funnels mounted at aft-end of aft superstructure.

SPECIFICATION

Displacement, tons: 35,087 standard, 106,692 full.

Length, feet (meters): 785 (239.3) oa.

Beam, feet (meters): 164 (50) oa.

Draft, feet (meters): 36 (11).

Speed, knots: 15.

Ranges, miles: 9,500 at 15 kts.

Complement: 250 (19 Officers, 231 Enlisted).

ARMAMENT

Guns: 12 x .50-in cal/12.7mm MG.

AIR SUPPORT

Helicopters: 4 x MH-60R Seahawk.

Runnymede

US Navy Photo

Class: Runnymede (LCU)

Country of Origin: America

Operators: America

Active: 35

Name (Pennant Number):
RUNNYMEDE (2001), KENNESAW
MOUNTAIN (2002), MAXON (2003),
ALDIE (2004), BRANDY STATION
(2005), BRISTOE STATION (2006),
BROAD RUN (2007), BUENA VISTA
(2008), CALABOZA (2009), CEDAR RUN
(2010), CHICKAHOMINY (2011),
CHICKASAW BAYOU (2012),
CHURUBUSCO (2013), COAMO (2014),
CONTRERAS (2015), CORINTH (2016),
EL CANEY (2017), FIVE FORKS (2018),
FORT DONELSON (2019), FORT
MCHENRY (2020), GREAT BRIDGE
(2021), HARPERS FERRY (2022),
HOBKIRK (2023), HORMIGUEROS
(2024), MALVERN HILL (2025),
MATAMOROS (2026),
MECHANICSVILLE (2027),
MISSIONARY RIDGE (2028), MOLINO
DEL REY (2029), MONTERREY (2030),
NEW ORLEANS (2031), PALO ALTO
(2032), PAULUS HOOK (2033),
PERRYVILLE (2034), PORT HUDSON
(2035).

RECOGNITION FEATURES

- High bow with split gate for roll-on/roll-off transport, with break after forecastle to maindeck.
- Bridge superstructure fitted at stern.
- Wire mast mounted atop lattice, atop forecastle.
- Two navigation radars mounted atop bridge, second wire mast mounted after bridge atop aft superstructure.

Note: Cargo capacity for 24 standard 20-foot shipping containers.

Draft, feet (meters): 1'5" (0.44), 2'7" (0.79) max.

Speed, knots: 11.5.

Range, miles: 4,500 at 11.5 kts (light).

Complement: 13 (2 Officers, 11 Enlisted).

SENSORS
Navigation: SPS-64(V)2.

SPECIFICATION
Displacement, tons: 672 light, 1,102 full.

Length, feet (meters): 53' (16.16) oa.

Beam, feet (meters): 12'10" (3.9) oa.

CAPACITY
Cargo, tons: 350.

Vehicles: 5 M1A1 MBT.

San Antonio

Class: San Antonio (LPD)

Country of Origin: America	
Operators: America	

Active: 12 + 1 fitting out

Building: 2

Name (Pennant Number): (Flight I) SAN ANTONIO (17), NEW ORLEANS (18), MESA VERDE (10), GREEN BAY (20), NEW YORK (21), SAN DIEGO (22), ANCHORAGE (23), ARLINGTON (24), SOMERSET (25), JOHN P. MURTHA (26), PORTLAND (27), FORT LAUDERDALE (28), RICHARD M. MCCOOL JR. (29), (Flight II) HARRISBURG (30), PITTSBURGH (31), PHILADELPHIA (32).

SPECIFICATION

Displacement, tons: 25,000 full.

Length, feet (meters): 684 (208.5) oa.

Beam, feet (meters): 105 (31.9) oa.

Draft, feet (meters): 23 (7).

Speed, knots: 22.

Complement:441 (33 Officers, 411 Enlisted).

ARMAMENT

Missiles: 2 x 8 (16) VLS for RIM-162 ESSM; 2 x 21 (42) Mk 49 RAM.

Guns: 2 x 30mm Mk 46 Bushmaster CIWS. 4 x .50-in cal./12.7mm MG.

Electronic: AN/SLQ-32 EW suite.

Decoys: Mk 36 SRBOC, Mk 53 Nulka, AN/SLQ-25 Nixie torpedo decoy.

RECOGNITION FEATURES

- Level forecastle with hull chine running bow to stern.
- Superstructure sheer to sides, with stealthy characteristics.
- SAM VLS battery forward of bridge.
- 2 black-tipped funnels with 4 exhausts, offset port and starboard atop island.
- 2 pyramidal enclosed masts atop superstructure.
- Crane mounted between funnels.
- Aft flight deck connected to two hangers in aft end of superstructure.

Note: Well deck and stern gate allows for LCAC launch and amphibious assault.

SENSORS

Air search: AN/SPS-48G; (29+) Enterprise Air Surveillance Radar (EASR).

Surface search/Navigation: AN/SPS-73(V)3.

Fire control: AN/SPQ-9B.

AIR SUPPORT

Helicopters: 4 x MH-60R Seahawk.

CAPACITY

Troops: 691.

Vehicles: 2 LCAC.

Whidbey Island

US Air Force Photo

Class: Whidbey Island (LSD)

Country of Origin: America

Operators: America

Active: 6

Name (Pennant Number): GERMANTOWN (42), GUNSTON HALL (44), COMSTOCK (45), TORTUGA (46), RUSHMORE (47), ASHLAND (48).

SPECIFICATION

Displacement, tons: 16,750.

Length, feet (meters): 609'6" (185.8) oa.

Beam, feet (meters): 84 (25.6) oa.

Draft, feet (meters): 20'6" (6.3).

Speed, knots: 22.

Range, miles: 8,000 at 18 kts.

Complement: 349 (22 Officers, 327 Enlisted).

ARMAMENT

Missiles: SAM – 2 x Mk 49 RAM.

Guns: 2 x Mk 15 Phalanx CIWS, 6 x .50-in cal/12.7mm. MG, 2 x 25mm Mk 38 Bushmaster gun.

Decoys: 6 x Mk 36 SRBOC, AN/SLQ-25 Nixie torpedo decoy.

SENSORS

Air search: AN/SPS-49(V)5.

Surface search: AN/SPS-67V.

Navigation: AN/SPS-64(V)9.

RECOGNITION FEATURES

- Level forecastle with forward wire mast at bow.
- Rectangular superstructure forward of midships, sheer to sides.
- Lattice mainmast supports radar aerials mid-superstructure.
- Aft-sloped funnel at aft end of superstructure.
- 2 CIWS mountings atop main superstructure, 1 forward of bridge, 1 immediately forward of funnel.
- RAM launchers atop bridge roof and at aft end of superstructure.
- 2 cranes mounted after funnel on extended quarterdeck.
- Flight deck supports helicopter operations, but no hangar onboard.

Note: Whidbey Island-class LSD is very similar in appearance to Harpers Ferry-class LSD. Harpers Ferry has RAM launcher mounted forward of bridge and CIWS mounted atop bridge.

AIR SUPPORT

Helicopters: 2 x SH-60B or MH-60R Seahawk.

CAPACITY

Troops: 500.

Vehicles: 4 LCAC or 3 LCU or 10 LCM-8 or 21 LCM-6, or 64 LVTP.

Yubei

Class: Yubei Type 074A (LCU)

Country of Origin: China	
Operators: China	

Active: 14

Name (Pennant Number): (3128), (3129), (3232), (3233), (3234), (3235), (3215), (3316), (3317), (3318), (3318), (3357), (3358), (3359).

SPECIFICATION

Displacement, tons: 650 standard, 800 full.

Length, feet (meters): 191'7'" (58.4) oa.

Beam, feet (meters): 34'1'" (10.4) oa.

Draft, feet (meters): 8'10'" (2.7).

Speed, knots: 18.

Complement: 56.

ARMAMENT

Missiles: 2 x 40 (80) 122mm Type 81H MRLS.

Guns: 2 x 25mm Type 61 dual gun.

RECOGNITION FEATURES

- Distinctive wide, high bow with door for roll-on/roll-off transport, with break after forecastle to level, open deck.
- Bridge superstructure fitted starboard-side after midships, with starboard side sheer to hull.
- Missile tubes mounted forward bridge.
- Dual gun turrets mounted on forecastle, port and starboard.
- Enclosed mast mounted atop superstructure, aft of bridge.

Note: Bow doors enable roll-on/roll-off loading/unloading capability.

CAPACITY

Cargo, tons: 1,000.

Troops: 200.

Vehicles: 10 fighting vehicles.

Yudeng

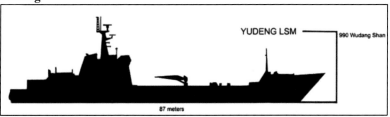

YUDENG LSM — 990 Wudang Shan

87 meters

Class: Yudeng Type 073III (LSM)

US Navy Photo

Country of Origin: China	
Operators: China	

Active: 1

Name (Pennant Number): (990).

SPECIFICATION

Displacement, tons: 1,850 full.

Length, feet (meters): 285'2" (87) oa.

Beam, feet (meters): 42'8'" (13) oa.

Draft, feet (meters): 12'6" (3.8).

Speed, knots: 14.

Range, miles: 1,500 at 14 kts.

Complement: 40.

ARMAMENT

Missiles: 2 x 40 (80) 122mm Type 81H MRLS.

Guns: 2 x 37mm Type 76 dual gun.

RECOGNITION FEATURES

- High bow with split gate for roll-on/roll-off transport, with break after forecastle to maindeck.
- Bridge superstructure fitted after midships, with covered passage ways port and starboard allowing transit from maindeck to quarterdeck.
- Tall "T" shaped mainmast atop superstructure after bridge supports navigation, radar aerials.
- 1 dual gun turret mounted on forecastle, 1 on quarterdeck.

Note: Yudeng is a smaller version of the retired Yukan-class LSM.

CAPACITY

Cargo, tons: 250.

Troops: 180-500.

Vehicles: 6 armored fighting vehicles.

Yuhai

Class: Yuhai Type 074 (LSM)

Tksteven Photo (CC BY 3.0)

Country of Origin: China	
Operators: China	

Active: 12

Name (Pennant Number): (3111), (3112), (3113), (3115), (3116), (3117), (3244), (5576), (7593), (7594), (7595), 7596).

SPECIFICATION

Displacement, tons: 650 standard, 800 full.

Length, feet (meters): 191'7'" (58.4) oa.

Beam, feet (meters): 34'1'" (10.4) oa.

Draft, feet (meters): 8'10'" (2.7).

Speed, knots: 18.

Complement: 56.

ARMAMENT

Guns: 2 x 25mm Type 61 dual gun, 1 x 37mm

Type 76 dual gun.

RECOGNITION FEATURES

- High bow with split gate for roll-on/roll-off transport, with break after forecastle to maindeck.
- Bridge superstructure fitted after midships, with covered passage ways port and starboard allowing transit from maindeck to quarterdeck.
- Mainmast atop superstructure after bridge supports navigation radar aerial.
- Lifeboats davits after superstructure.
- 2 Type 61 dual gun turrets mounted on superstructure, forward bridge.
- 1 Type 76 dual gun turret mounted on forecastle.

CAPACITY

Troops: 250.

Vehicles: 2 armored fighting vehicles.

Yunshu

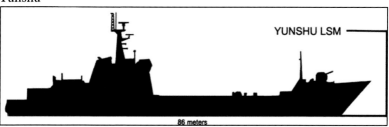

YUNSHU LSM

86 meters

US Navy Photo

Class: Yunshu Type 073A (LSM)

Country of Origin: China

Operators: China

Active: 10

Name (Pennant Number): SHENGZHOU (941), LUSHAN (942), MONSANTO (943), YUSHAN (944), HUASHAN (045), SONGSHAN (946), (947), (948), HENGSHAN (949), TAISHAN (950).

SPECIFICATION

Displacement, tons: 1,460 standard, 2,000 full.

Length, feet (meters): 285'5" (87) oa.

Beam, feet (meters): 41'4" (12.6) oa.

Draft, feet (meters): 7'6" (2.3).

Speed, knots: 17.

Range, miles: 1,500 at 14 kts.

Complement: 70.

ARMAMENT

Missiles: 2 x 40 (80) 122mm Type 81H MRLS.

Guns: 1 x 37mm Type 76F dual gun.

RECOGNITION FEATURES

- High bow with break after forecastle to maindeck.
- Floodable bow gate supports roll-on/roll-off capability and amphibious assault.
- Bridge superstructure fitted after midships, with covered passage ways port and starboard allowing transit from maindeck to quarterdeck.
- Mainmast atop superstructure after bridge supports navigation radar aerial.
- Single black-tipped funnel after superstructure.
- Lifeboats on starboard-side davits after superstructure.
- 1 Type 76F dual gun turret mounted on forecastle.
- Pole fitted after gun turret on forecastle.

CAPACITY

Cargo, tons: 1,000.

Troops: 500.

Vehicles: 6 armored fighting vehicles.

Yuting I/II/III

Class: Yuting I/II/III Type 072II/072III/072A (LST)

Ministry of Defense of Russia Photo

Country of Origin: China

Operators: China

Active: 28, (I) 3, (II) 10), (III) 15.

Name (Pennant Number): (I) DONGTING SHAN (931), HELAN SHAN (932), LIUPAN SHAN (933); (II) YANDANG SHAN (908), JIHUA SHAN (909), HUANGGANG SHAN (910), DANXIA SHAN (934), XUEFENG SHAN (935), HAIYANG SHAN (936), QINGCHENG SHAN (937), PUTUO SHAN (939), TIANTAI SHAN (940), EMEI SHAN (991); (III) TIANZHU SHAN (911), DAQING SHAN (912), BAXIAN SHAN (913), WUYI SHAN (914), CULAI SHAN (915), TIANMU SHAN (916), WUTAI SHAN (917), HUADING SHAN (992), LUOXIAO SHAN (993), DAIYUN SHAN (994), WANYANG SHAN (995), LAOTIE SHAN (996), LUHUA SHAN (997), DABIE SHAN (981), TAIHANG SHAN (982).

SPECIFICATION

Displacement, tons: (II) 3,430 standard, 4,800 full; (III) 7,200 full.

Length, feet (meters): 392 (119.5) oa.

Beam, feet (meters): 53'10" (16.4) oa.

Draft, feet (meters): 9'2" (2.8).

Speed, knots: (I) 14, (II) 18.

Range, miles: 3,000 at 14 kts.

Complement: (I) 104; (II) 120.

RECOGNITION FEATURES

- High bow with break after forecastle to maindeck.
- Floodable bow gate supports roll-on/roll-off capability and amphibious assault.
- Bridge superstructure fitted after midships, with sides sheer to hull.
- Enclosed mainmast atop superstructure after bridge.
- Single black-tipped funnel sloped up and aft, fitted after superstructure.
- Lifeboats on port and starboard davits atop aft superstructure.
- 1 Type 76 dual gun turret mounted on forecastle, 2 on port and starboard, forward-side of superstructure, forward of bridge.
- Pole fitted after gun turret on forecastle.
- Elevated flight deck after funnel.

ARMAMENT

Guns: (I) 3 x 37mm Type 76 H/PJ76F dual gun; (II) 4 x 37mm Type 76 H/PJ76F dual gun.

AIR SUPPORT

Helicopters: (I) 1 x Z-8 Super Frelon; (II) 2 x Z-8 Super Frelon.

CAPACITY

Cargo, tons: (II) 500; (II) 800.

Troops: 250.

Vehicles: 4 LCVP, 10 armored fighting vehicles

Yuzhao

Class: Yuzhao Type 071 (LPD)

US Navy Photo

Country of Origin: China

Operators: China

Active: 8

Name (Pennant Number): LONGHU SHAN (980), QILIAN SHAN (985), SIMING SHAN (986), WUZHI SHAN (987), YIMENG SHAN (988), CHANGBAI SHAN (989), KUNLUN SHAN (998), JINGGANG SHAN (999).

SPECIFICATION

Displacement, tons: 20,000 standard, 25,000 full.

Length, feet (meters): 689 (210) oa.

Beam, feet (meters): 91'10" (28) oa.

Draft, feet (meters): 23 (7).

Speed, knots: 25.

Range, miles: 6,000 at 18 kts.

Complement: 175.

ARMAMENT

Guns:1 x 3-in/76mm PJ-26 gun, 4 x 30mm H/PJ-13 CIWS.

Decoys: 4 x 18 (72) Type 726 decoy/chaff launchers.

SENSORS

Air search: Type 363S 2D, Type 364/SR-64 Seagull C 2D.

Air/surface search: Type 360 Seagull-S.

Navigation: RM-1290.

Fire control: Type 344 (CIWS), LR-66C (gun), Type 345 (SAM)).

AIR SUPPORT

Helicopters: 4 x Z-8 Super Frelon.

RECOGNITION FEATURES

- High bow with hull chine that runs from bow to stern.
- Enclosed mast atop superstructure, after bridge supports Type 360 Seagull-S radar.
- 2 CIWS mountings fitted at aft end of superstructure port and starboard.
- 3-in gun mounted in B position.
- Small boats fitted on davits, port and starboard, forward of midships.
- Large stern flight deck able to support 2 helicopter launches or recoveries simultaneously.

Note: LCACs are launched from floodable stern gate.

CAPACITY

Troops: 800.

Vehicles: 4 MBTs, 15-20 amphibious armored vehicles, 4 Type 726 Yuyi LCACs.

Aist

Class: Aist Project 12321 Dzheyran (LCAC)

Country of Origin: Soviet Union	
Operators: Russia	
Active: 1	
Name (Pennant Number): MDK-18 (608)	

US Department of the Army Photo

SPECIFICATION

Displacement, tons: 298 standard, 355 full.

Length, feet (meters): 156'10" (47.8) oa.

Beam, feet (meters): 57'5" (17.5) oa.

Draft, feet (meters): 1' (0.3).

Speed, knots: 70 light, 50 loaded.

Range, miles: 100 at 45 kts, 208 at 40 kts.

Complement: 21 (3 Officers, 18 Enlisted).

ARMAMENT

Missiles: SAM – 2 x 4 (8) Fasta-4m/SA-N-8
Gremlin.

Guns: 2 x 2 (4) 365 cal/30mm AK-230 CIWS.

Decoys: 2 x 16 (32) PK-16.

SENSORS

Navigation: Mius / Spin Trough.

Fire control: MR-104 Rys/Drum Tilt.

RECOGNITION FEATURES

- Air cushion-inflated hovercraft with forward extended bow.
- Four distinctive propellers mounted after midships in pairs, port and starboard.
- Bridge mounted forward.
- Twin direction vanes mounted at stern, aligned with forward pairs of propellers.

Note: Bow opens for roll-on/roll-off loading capability.

CAPACITY

Cargo, tons: 74.

Troops: 220.

Vehicles: 2 MBT or 4 PT-76 or 5 BTR.

Alligator

Class: Alligator Project 1171 Tapir (LST)

Country of Origin: Soviet Union

Operators: Russia

Active: 3

Name (Pennant Number): NIKOLAY VILKOV (081), ORSK (148), NIKOLAY FILCHENKOV (152).

SPECIFICATION

Displacement, tons: 2,885 standard, 4,946 full.

Length, feet (meters): 371'1" (113.1) oa.

Beam, feet (meters): 51'2" (15.6) oa.

Draft, feet (meters): 12'2" (3.7).

Speed, knots: 17.

Range, miles: 6,312 at 17 kts, 9,150 at 9 kts.

Complement: 77 (6 Officers, 9 Warrant, 62

Enlisted).

ARMAMENT

Missiles: SAM – 3 x 4 (12) MTU-4S launcher

for 9K34 Strela-3/SA-N-8 Gremlin, (081, 152)

SSM - 40 x MS-73 launcher for (40) 122 mm

9M22 A-215 Grad-M.

Guns: 1 x 57mm AK-257 twin gun, (081, 152) 2

x 25mm 2M-3M twin gun.

Grenades: (081) 2 x 7 (14) 55mm MRG-1

Ogonyok.

SENSORS

Navigation: Don, (150) MR-231 PAL.

Fire control: (081, 152) PS-73 Groza-1171

(SSM).

Sonars: MG-7 Braslet anti-saboteur.

CAPACITY

RECOGNITION FEATURES

- High bow with high freeboard running to superstructure after midships.
- Superstructure sited after midships.
- 57mm twin gun turret mounted in B position, forward of superstructure, after midships.
- 3 cargo cranes; 1 after forecastle, 1 at midships, and 1 after superstructure at stern.
- Lifeboats mounted on davits port and starboard after bridge, atop superstructure.

Note: Bow doors open for roll-on/roll-off discharge of cargo, troops, and vehicles.

Cargo, tons: 1,000.

Troops: (148, 150) 313, (081, 152) 440.

Vehicles: 20 MBT or 47 BTR or 52 trucks.

Dyugon

Class: Dyugon Project 2182 (LCU)

Country of Origin: Russia	
Operators: Russia	

Active: 5

Name (Pennant Number): ATAMAN
PLAKHOV, IVAN KATRSOV, DENIS
PLATOV, MICHMAN LERMONTO,
LEYTENANT RIMSKIY-KORSAKOV.

SPECIFICATION
Displacement, tons: 280 full.

Length, feet (meters): 147'8" (45) oa.

Beam, feet (meters): 28'3" (8.6) oa.

Draft, feet (meters): 7'3" (2.2).

Speed, knots: 50.

Complement: 6.

ARMAMENT
Guns: 2 x 14.5mm MTPU Zhalo MG.

SENSORS
Navigation: Don, (150) MR-231 PAL.

Fire control: (081, 152) PS-73 Groza-1171
(SSM).

Sonars: MG-7 Braslet anti-saboteur.

CAPACITY
Cargo, tons: 140.

Troops: 90.

Vehicles: 3 MBT or 5 BTR.

RECOGNITION FEATURES
- Forward-slanted flat bow, opens to allow RO/RO loading and unloading.
- Open well-deck runs from bow to bridge superstructure at stern.
- Bridge superstructure mounted after midships.
- Enclosed, aft-angled mast mounted atop bridge.

Note: Derived from Serna-class, although twice as long.

Ivan Gren

Class: Ivan Gren Project 11711 (LST)

Ministry of Defense of Russia Photo

Country of Origin: Russia	
Operators: Russia	
Active: 2	
Building: 2	

Name (Pennant Number): IVAN GREN (010), PYOTR MORGUNOV (117), VLADIMIR ANDREEV (---), VASILY TRUSHIN (---).

SPECIFICATION
Displacement, tons: 5,000 standard, 6,000 full.

Length, feet (meters): 393'8" (120) oa.

Beam, feet (meters): 54'2" (16.5) oa.

Draft, feet (meters): 11'10" (3.6).

Speed, knots: 18.

Range, miles: 3,500 at 16 kts.

Complement: 100.

ARMAMENT
Missiles: SAM – 1 x 9K38 Igla launcher for (8) 9M39/SA-N-10 Grouse.

Guns: 1 x 30mm AK-630M Duet CIWS, 2 x 30mm AK-630M CIWS, 2 x 14.5mm MTPU-1 Zhalo MG.

Decoys: KT-308-04 launcher for Prosvet-M decoys.

SENSORS
Air/surface search: MR-352 Pozitiv.

Navigation: MR-231 Pal, MR-231-2 Liman.

Fire control: 5P-10-03 Laska (CIWS).

AIR SUPPORT
Helicopters: 2 x Ka-29 (ASW) Helix-B.

RECOGNITION FEATURES
- Blunt front end to high bow.
- 2 superstructures; bridge superstructure fitted forward midships.
- Pozitiv radar aerial fitted atop mast on bridge superstructure.
- Distinctive "T" shaped mast mounted forward on aft superstructure.
- CIWS mounted in B position, forward bridge superstructure.
- Crane mounted midships, between bridge and aft superstructures.
- Flight deck at stern supports 2 ASW helicopters housed in hangar in aft superstructure.

CAPACITY
Cargo, tons: 1,500.

Troops: 300.

Vehicles: 13 MBT or 36 BTR.

Lebed

Class: Lebed Project 1206 Kalmar (LCMA)

Country of Origin: Soviet Union

Operators: Russia

Active: 1

Name (Pennant Number): MDK-235

SPECIFICATION

Displacement, tons: 108 standard, 114 full.

Length, feet (meters): 80'1" (24.6) oa.

Beam, feet (meters): 35'5" (10.8) oa.

Draft, feet (meters): 4'3" (1.3).

Speed, knots: 70.

Range, miles: 100 at 50 kts.

Complement: 6 (2 Officers, 4 Enlisted).

ARMAMENT

Guns: 1 x 12.7mm Utes-M MG.

RECOGNITION FEATURES

- Air cushion-inflated hovercraft.
- Two ringed propellers mounted forward of stern, port and starboard.
- Bridge integrated into hull, forward.
- Twin direction vanes mounted at stern, aligned with ringed-propellers.

SENSORS

Navigation: Kivach-2.

CAPACITY

Cargo, tons: 37.

Troops: 120.

Vehicles: 1 MBT or 2 PT-76.

Ondatra

Class: Ondatra Project 1176 Akula (LCM)

Country of Origin: Soviet Union

Operators: Russia

Active: 14

Name (Pennant Number): D-704 (640), D-70 (677), D-464 (590), D-465 (746), D-295 (542), D-325 (799), D-148 (578), D-365 (--), D-182 (533), D-185 (642), D-57 (675), NIKOLAI RUBTSOV (555), D-184 (184), D-106 (543)

Ministry of Defense of Ukraine Photo

RECOGNITION FEATURES

- Forward-slanted flat bow, opens to allow RO/RO loading and unloading.
- Open well-deck runs from bow to bridge superstructure at stern, may be covered by tarp.
- Bridge mounted at stern.
- Wire mast mounted atop bridge.

SPECIFICATION

Displacement, tons: 90 standard, 107 full.

Length, feet (meters): 80'5" (24.5) oa.

Beam, feet (meters): 19'8" (6) oa.

Draft, feet (meters): 5'1" (1.55).

Speed, knots: 11.5.

Range, miles: 330 at 10 kts, 500 at 5 kts.

Complement: 5 (5 Enlisted).

SENSORS

Navigation: Mius / Spin Trough.

CAPACITY

Cargo, tons: 50.

Troops: 20.

Vehicles: 1 MBT.

Pomornik

Class: Pomornik Project 12322 Zubr (LCAC)

Ministry of Defense of Russia Photo

Country of Origin: Soviet Union

Operators: Russia, China

Active: 6; (Russia) 2, (China) 6.

Name (Pennant Number): (China) 3325-3330; (Russia) EVGENIY KOCHESHKOV (770), MORDOVIYA (782)

SPECIFICATION

Displacement, tons: 500 standard, 550 full.

Length, feet (meters): 188 (57.3) oa.

Beam, feet (meters): 84 (25.6) oa.

Draft, feet (meters): 5'3" (1.6).

Speed, knots: 63.

Complement: 27 (4 Officers, 23 Enlisted).

ARMAMENT

Missiles: SAM – 2 MTU-2 Igla-1M launcher for (8) 9M39/SA-N-10 Grouse.

Guns: 2 x 30mm AK-630M CIWS.

Flame thrower: 2 x 22 MS-227 launchers for (44) A-22 Ogon.

Mines: 58 (instead of troops).

Electronic: MP-411 ESM system.

RECOGNITION FEATURES

- Air cushion-inflated hovercraft with outboard-sloped catamaran hull.
- Three distinctive ring shrouds for air propellers mounted at stern.
- Lattice mast mounted atop enclosed mast, at aft end of superstructure.
- 2 CIWS turrets mounted port and starboard, forward bridge, after forecastle.

Note: Bow opens for roll-on/roll-off loading capability.

SENSORS

Navigation: MR-244-3 Ekran-1, Lazur.

Fire control: DVU-3 (flame thrower), M-123-01 Vympel (gun).

CAPACITY

Cargo, tons: 150 maximum.

Troops: 140-360.

Vehicles: 3 MBT or 10 BTR or 8 BMP.

Ropucha

Class: Ropucha Project 775/II/III (LST)

Country of Origin: Soviet Union

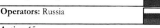

George Chernilevsky Photo

Operators: Russia

Active: 15

Name (Pennant Number): (I)
OLENEGORSKIY GORNYAK (012),
KONDOPOGA (027), ALEXANDR
OTRAKOVSKIY (031), (II) GEORGIY
POBEDONOSETS (016), ADMIRAL
NEVELSKOY (055), OSLYABLYA (066),
KALININGRAD (102), ALEXANDR
SHABALIN (110), MINSK (127),
NOVOCHERKASSK (142), YAMAL (156),
TSEZAR KUNIKOV (158) (III) PERESVET
(077), KOROLEV (130), AZOV (151).

SPECIFICATION

Displacement, tons: 2,768 standard, 4,012 full.

Length, feet (meters): 369'5" (112.6) oa.

Beam, feet (meters): 49'3" (15) oa.

Draft, feet (meters): 13'5" (4.1).

Speed, knots: 17.6.

Complement: 98 (17 Officers, 81 Enlisted).

ARMAMENT

Missiles: (II/III) SAM – 2 x 4 (8) 9K38 Igla for
9M39/SA-N-10 Grouse, (016, 102) SSM – 2 x
40 (80) MS-73 launcher for (40) 122 mm 9M22
A-215 Grad-M.

Guns: (I/II) 2 x 3-in/57mm AK-725 gun, (III) 1
x 3.9-in/76mm AK-176M gun, 2 x 30mm AK-
630M CIWS; (012, 077, 110, 156) 2 x 2 x 45mm
21-KM gun.

Decoys: (III) 2 x KL-101 launchers for PK-16.

RECOGNITION FEATURES

- High, squared forward bow, with maindeck running from bow to stern.
- Superstructure centered after midships.
- Pole mast atop bridge roof.
- Lattice mainmast atop superstructure, aft of bridge
- Square funnel mounted in superstructure after lattice mainmast.
- (I/II) 3-in guns mounted fore and aft; (III) 3.9-in gun mounted forward, 2 CIWS mounted after superstructure, port and starboard.

Note: Bow and stern doors open for roll-on/roll-off discharge of cargo, troops, and vehicles. Long-sliding hatch above the forecastle allows crane access to vehicle deck.

SENSORS

Air/surface search: (I/II) MR-302 Rubka, (III) MR-352 Pozitiv-E.

Navigation: (077) MP-212 Vaygach, (110) MR-212/201 Vaygach-U, (127) Mius.

Fire control: Groza-1171 (SSM); (I/II) M-103 Bars, (III)MR-123 Vympel-A (gun).

CAPACITY

Cargo, tons: 500.

Troops: 340; 312; 150

Vehicles: 10 MBTs; 3 MBTs, 8 armored vehicles, 4 trucks; 12 PT-76 or 20 trucks.

Serna

Class: Serna Project 1177 (LCM)

Country of Origin: Soviet Union

Operators: Russia

Active: 12

Name (Pennant Number): D-67 (747), D-156 (723), D-131 (722), D-172 (724), D-144 (665), D-56 (721), ALEXEY BARINOV (791), IVAN PASKO (792), CASPIAN FLOTILIA (809), D-(810), D-199 (659), ANDREY IVANOV (650)

RECOGNITION FEATURES

- Forward-slanted flat bow, opens to allow RO/RO loading and unloading.
- Open well-deck runs from bow to bridge superstructure at stern.
- Wire mast mounted after bridge atop superstructure.

SPECIFICATION

Displacement, tons: 53 light, 105 full.

Length, feet (meters): 84'2" (25.65) oa.

Beam, feet (meters): 19'2" (5.85) oa.

Draft, feet (meters): 5' (1.52).

Speed, knots: 30.

Range, miles: 100 at 30 kts loaded, 600 at 30 kts when half-full.

Complement: 4.

ARMAMENT

Missiles: SAM – 1 x MTU-4S launcher for 9K34 Strela-3/SA-N-8 Gremlin.

Guns: 3 x 7.62mm PKMB MG

SENSORS

Navigation: Mius / Spin Trough.

CAPACITY

Cargo, tons: 50.

Troops: 100.

Vehicles: 1 MBT or BTR.

Cruisers

Ticonderoga

US Navy Photo

Class: Ticonderoga (CG)

Country of Origin: America

Operators: America

Active: 13

Retired: 9

Name (Pennant Number): (Active) ANTIETAM (54), LEYTE GULF (55), PHILIPPINE SEA (58), PRINCETON (59), NORMANDY (60), CHANCELLORSVILLE (62), COWPENS (63), GETTYSBURG (64), CHOSIN (65), SHILOH (67), VICKSBURG (69), LAKE ERIE (70), CAPE ST GEORGE (71), (Retired) BUNKER HILL (52), MOBILE BAY (53), SAN JACINTO (56), LAKE CHAMPLAIN (57), MONTEREY (61), HUE CITY (66), ANZIO (68), VELLA GULF (72), PORT ROYAL (73)

SPECIFICATION

Displacement, tons: 9,600.

Length, feet (meters): 565'10" (172.5) oa.

Beam, feet (meters): 55 (16.8) oa.

Draft, feet (meters): 31'6" (9.6).

Speed, knots: 32.5.

Complement: 330 (30 Officers, 300 Enlisted).

ARMAMENT

Missiles: SLCM – 8 x RGM-84 Harpoon, (122) Mk 41 VLS launchers containing: A/S - RUM-139A VL-ASROC; SAM - RIM-66M-5 SM-2, RIM-156A S-2ER, RIM-161 SM-3, RIM-162 ESSM, RIM174A Standard ERAM; SLCM - BGM-109 Tomahawk.

Guns: 2 x Phalanx CIWS Block 1B, 2-4 x .50-in cal./12.7mm MG, 2 x 25mm Mk 38 gun, 2 x 5-in/127mm Mark 45 Mod 4 gun.

Torpedoes: 2 x Mk 32 triple torpedo tubes 12.75 in (324 mm).

Electronic: AN/SLQ-32 EW suite.

RECOGNITION FEATURES

- High bow with break in sides after forecastle.
- One 5-in gun mounting on forecastle and one on quarterdeck.
- Two VLS batteries, between forward turret and bridge superstructure, one at aft break before quarterdeck.
- Forward bridge superstructure fitted forward of midships, with lattice mast atop bridge roof to support fire control radar.
- Twin funnels with 3 exhausts each. Forward funnel with 2 exhausts forward smaller funnel, aft funnel with three exhausts fitted on forward edge of aft superstructure.
- Lattice mainmast fitted between funnels at midships.

Decoys: Mk 36 SRBOC, AN/SLQ-25 Nixie torpedo decoy.

SENSORS

Air search: AN/SPS-49.

Surface search: AN/SPS-73.

Navigation: AN/SPY-1A/B multi-function radar.

Fire control: AN/SPQ-9 (gun), AN/SPG-62.

Sonars: AN/SQS-53B/C/D active, AN/SQR-19 TACTASS, AN/SQR-19B, ITAS, MFTA passive, AN/SQQ-28 LAMPS sonar.

AIR SUPPORT

Helicopters: 2 x SH-60B or MH-60R Seahawk LAMPS.

Renhai

Class: Renhai Type 055 (CG)

Ministry of Defense of Japan Photo

Country of Origin: China	
Operators: China	

Active: 8

Building: 2

Name (Pennant Number): NANCHANG (101), LHASA (102), ANSHAN (103), WUXI (104), DALIAN (105), YAN'AN (106), ZUNYI (107), XIANYANG (108), --- (109), ---- (110)

SPECIFICATION

Displacement, tons: 13,000.

Length, feet (meters): 590'7" (180) oa.

Beam, feet (meters): 65'8" (20) oa.

Draft, feet (meters): 21'8" (6.6).

Speed, knots: 30+.

Range (miles): 5,000 at 18 kts.

Complement: 300.

ARMAMENT

Missiles: SAM – 1 x 24 cell HHQ-10, (112) VLS tubes (1 x 64x; 1 x 48x) containing A/S - Yu-8A ASROC; SAM – HQ-9B; SSM – YJ-18A.

Guns: 1 x H/PJ 130 mm gun, 2 x H/PJ11 CIWS.

Torpedoes: 2 x 3 torpedo tubes for Yu-7 torpedo.

Electronic: ESM with EW jammers.

Decoys: Type 726-4 launchers.

SENSORS

Air search: Type 346B Dragon Eye, X-band radar.

Surface search: Type 360S Seagull air-surface.

Navigation: Type 360S Seagull air-surface.

RECOGNITION FEATURES

- Flared hull with enclosed bow (anchor chains hidden belowdecks).
- Enclosed bridge atop sloped superstructure.
- Pyramidal mainmast.
- H/LJG 346B Dragon Eye radar mounted below bridge on superstructure.
- H/PJ11 CIWS mounted on sponson before bridge superstructure.
- 2 dual funnels enclosed in aft part of superstructure.
- 64 x VLS cells forward of bridge and aft of 130mm gun.
- 48 x VLS cells aft of bridge, forward of the double hangar.
- HHQ-10 SAM launcher mounting on aft structure, forward of flight deck.

Note: China considers the Type 055 to be a destroyer, but its size and armament have caused Western countries to classify it as a cruiser.

Fire control: Type 342, Type 344.

Sonars: hull-mounted sonar (bow); towed array sonar; VDS.

AIR SUPPORT

Helicopters: 2 x Z-18 Super Frelon or Z-9 Haitun.

Kirov

Class: Kirov Project 1144 Orlan (CG)

Country of Origin: Soviet Union

Operators: Russia

Active: 1 + 1 in refit

Name (Pennant Number): ADMIRAL NAKHIMOV (080), PYOTR VELIKIY (099)

SPECIFICATION

Displacement, tons: 24,300 (standard), 28,000 (full).

Length, feet (meters): 826'9" (252) oa.

Beam, feet (meters): 93'6" (28.5) oa.

Draft, feet (meters): 29'10" (9.1).

Speed, knots: 32.

Range (miles): 14,000 at 30 kts.

Complement: 762 (101 Officers, 643 Enlisted, 18 Air Crew).

ARMAMENT

Missiles: A/S – 2 x RBU-1000 Smerch-3 305 mm ASROC rocket launchers; SAM – 8 x 8 (64) 3K95 Kinzhal/SA-N-9 Gauntlet; 6 x 8 (48) SA-N-6/S-300FM Fort-M; 6 x 8 (48) S-300F Fort; SSM – 20 x P-700 Granit/SS-N-19 Shipwreck.

Guns: 1 x twin AK-130 5.1in/130mm dual-purpose gun; 6 x CASD-N-1 Kashtan CIWS.

Torpedoes: 10 x 533mm torpedo tubes; Type 53 torpedo or SS-N-15 Starfish (ASW).

Decoys: 2 x ZIF-121 launchers; PK-2M decoys.

RECOGNITION FEATURES

- Raised raked bow with sloping forecastle.
- Deck breaks aft of superstructure, before flight deck.
- Mainmast mounted amidships, supports funnel and Top Pair radar aerial.
- Smaller mast mounted on superstructure aft of mainmast supports Top Plate and Top Dome radar aerials.
- 5.1-in twin gun mounted aft of superstructure, forward of flight deck.
- VLS cell battery fitted forward of superstructure, aft of forecastle

Note: Hangar located below flight deck.

SENSORS

Long range air search: Tomb Stone PESA.

Air search: MR-800 3D; MR-710 3D.

Surface search: MR-320M Topaz-V/Strut Pair.

Navigation: MR-231-3 Palm Frond; MR-232-2; MR-231-3.

Fire control: 3R41/Top Dome; MR-360 Cross Sword; 3P37 Hot Flash; MR-814 Kite Screech.

Sonars: MG-355 Horse Jaw LF hull-mounted; Horse Tail LF VDS, 2 x Anapa-M anti-saboteur.

AIR SUPPORT

Helicopters: 3 x Ka-27PL Helix or Ka-29 Helix B or Ka-31 Helix E

Slava

Class: Slava Project 1164 Atlant (CG)

Country of Origin: Soviet Union	
Operators: Russia	

Active: 2

Name (Pennant Number): VARYAG (011), MARSHAL USTINOV (055).

US Navy Photo

SPECIFICATION

Displacement, tons: 9,300 (standard), 11,490 (full).
Length, feet (meters): 611'7" (186.4) oa.
Beam, feet (meters): 68'3" (20.8) oa.
Draft, feet (meters): 27'7" (8.4).
Speed, knots: 32.
Range (miles): 8,070 at 18 kts, 2500 at 30 kts.
Complement: 485 (66 Officers, 419 Enlisted).

ARMAMENT

Missiles: SAM - 8 x 8 (64) S-300F/SA-N-6 Grumble; 2 x 20 (40) OSA-M/SA-N-4 Gecko; SSM – 8 x 2 (16) P-1000 Vulkan/SS-N-12 Sandbox.
Guns: 1 x twin AK-130 5.1in/130mm dual-purpose gun; 6 x AK-630 CIWS.
Torpedoes: 2 x 5 (10) 21"/533mm PTA-53-1134 torpedo tube quinteplet launcher with SET/Type 65-76 torpedoes.
Electronic: ESM - 2 x MP-150 Gurzuf-A, 2 x MP-152 Gurzuf B, MR-262 Ograda, MP-401 Start, MP-407 Start-2.
Decoys: 12 x KT-216 launchers with P-10 decoy, 2 x ZIF-121 launchers with PL-2M decoy.

SENSORS

Air search: air/surface search radar - MR-600 Voskhod/Top Sail, MR-710 Fregat-M/Top Plate; Fregat-M2 air-surface (Ustinov).

RECOGNITION FEATURES

- High bow and sloping forecastle, with deck break at flight deck.
- Pyramid mainmast mounted at aft end of bridge superstructure with horizontal lattice gantry, supports Top Plate Radar aerial.
- 5.1-in dual gun mounted on forecastle.
- 4 pairs of forward-angled SSM launchers mounted on port and starboard sides, starting at forecastle and ending after bridge superstructure.
- Secondary mast mounted before twin funnels supports Top Sail radar aerial.
- Top Dome radar mounted forward of flight deck.

Surface search: MR-650 Podberezovik 3D air-surface (Ustinov).
Navigation: MR-212 Vaygach; MR-231-3 (Moskva)
Fire control: MR-123-02/3 Bagira/Bass Tilt, MR-123 Vympel-A/Bass Tilt (Ustinov).
Sonars: MGK-335 Platina/Bull Nose hull-mounted; Zarya-SK (Ustinov).

AIR SUPPORT

Helicopters: 1 x Ka-27PL Helix or Ka-29 Helix B or Ka-31 Helix E

Destroyers

Arleigh Burke

Class: Arleigh Burke (DDG)

US Navy Photo

Country of Origin: America

Operators: America

Active: 73

Building: 10, 9 approved

Name (Pennant Number): Flight I – ARLEIGH
BURKE (51), BARRY (52), JOHN PAUL JONES (53),
CURTIS WILBUR (54), STOUT (55), JOHN S. MCCAIN
(56), MITSCHER (57), LABOON (58), RUSSELL (59),
PAUL HAMILTON (60), RAMAGE (61), FITZGERALD
(62), STETHEM (63), CARNEY (64), BENFOLD (65),
GONZALEZ (66), COLE (67), THE SULLIVANS (68),
MILIUS (69), HOPPER (70), ROSS (71); **Flight II** –
MAHAN (72), DECATUR (73), MCFAUL (74), DONALD
COOK (75), HIGGINS (76), O'KANE (77), PORTER (78);
Flight IIA – OSCAR AUSTIN (79), ROOSEVELT (80),
WINSTON S. CHURCHILL (81), LASSEN (82), HOWARD
(83), BULKELEY (84), MCCAMPBELL (85), SHOUP (86),
MASON (87), PREBLE (88), MUSTIN (89), CHAFEE (90),
PINCKNEY (91), MOMSEN (92), CHUNG-HOON (93),
NITZE (94), JAMES E. WILLIAMS (95), BAINBRIDGE
(96), HALSEY (97), FORREST SHERMAN (98),
FARRAGUT (99), GRIDLEY (101), SAMPSON (102),
TRUXTUN (103), STERETT (104), DEWEY (105),
STOCKDALE, GRAVELY (107), WAYNE E. MEYER
(108), JASON DUNHAM (109), WILLIAM P. LAWRENCE
(110), SPRUANCE (111), MICHAEL MURPHY (112),
JOHN FINN (113), RALPH JOHNSON (114), RAFAEL
PERALTA (115), THOMAS HUDNER (116), PAUL
IGNATIUS (117), DANIEL INOUYE (118), DELBERT D.
BLACK (119), CARL M. LEVIN (120), FRANK E.
PETERSEN JR. (121), JOHN BASILONE (122), LENAH H.
SUTCLIFFE HIGBEE (123), HARVEY C. BARNUM JR.
(124), PATRICK GALLAGHER (127); **Flight III** – JACK H.
LUCAS (125), LOUIS H. WILSON JR. (126), TED
STEVENS (128), JEREMIAH DENTON (129), WILLIAM
CHARETTE (130), GEORGE M. NEAL (131), QUENTIN
WALSH (132), SAM NUNN (133), JOHN E. KILMER (134),
THAD COCHRAN (135), RICHARD G. LUGAR (136),
JOHN F. LEHMAN (137), J. WILLIAM MIDDENDORF
(138), TELESFORO TRINIDAD (139), THOMAS G.
KELLY (140), --- (141), ---(142).

SPECIFICATION

Displacement, tons: 8,230-9,700.

Length, feet (meters): Flight I/II 505, Flight
IIA/III 509'6" (153.9/155.3) oa.

Beam, feet (meters): 59 (18) oa.

Draft, feet (meters): 30'6" (9.3).

Speed, knots: 30+.

Complement: Flight I 303, Flight IIA: 329.

ARMAMENT

Missiles: SSM – (Flight I/II) 2 x Mk 141 Harpoon,
(90) Mk 41 VLS, (Flight IIA/III) (96) MK 41 VLS
including A/S - RUM-139 ASROC; BMD- SM-
6/RIM-161; SAM – RIM-66M, RIM 174A SM-6
ERAM, (quadpacked) RIM-162 ESSM; SLCM -
BGM-109 TLAM.

Guns: 1 x Mk 45 5-in/127mm,(51-84) 2 x Phalanx
CIWS, (85+) 1 x Phalanx CIWS, 2 x M242
Bushmaster CG.

Torpedoes: 2 x triple (6) Mk 32 tubes with Mk
46/50/54.

Decoys: AN/SLQ-32(V)2 EW, AN/SLQ-25 Nixie,
MK 36 MOD 12, Mk 53 Nulka, AN/SLQ-39 Chaff
buoys.

SENSORS

Air search: (Flight I/II/IIA) AN/SPY-1, (Flight
III) AN/SPY-6.

Surface search: AN/SPS-67(V)2, AN/SPS-
73(V)12.

Fire control: AN/SPG-62.

Sonars: AN/SQQ-28 LAMPS III, AN/SQS-53C
array, AN/SQR-19 towed array.

AIR SUPPORT

Helicopters: Flight IIA/III 2 x MH-60B/R
Seahawk.

Zumwalt

Class: Zumwalt (DDG)

Country of Origin: America

Operators: America

Active: 2, 1 in sea trials

Name (Pennant Number): ZUMWALT (1000), MICHAEL MONSOOR (1001), LYNDON B. JOHNSON (1002)

SPECIFICATION

Displacement, tons: 15,656.

Length, feet (meters): 610 (185.9) oa.

Beam, feet (meters): 80'8" (24.6) oa.

Draft, feet (meters): 27'7" (8.4).

Speed, knots: 30.

Complement: 175 (147 + 28 air detachment).

ARMAMENT

Missiles: (80) Mk 57 VLS cells including A/S - RUM-139 ASROC; SAM – (quadpacked) RIM-162 ESSM; SSM – RGM-109E TLAM.

Guns: 2 x 6-in/155mm AGS (920 rounds), 2 x Mk 46 Bushmaster

RECOGNITION FEATURES

- Tumblehome hull design with forward protruding, down-sloped bow.
- Streamlined, inwardly slanted superstructure flush with hull to minimize radar cross-section.
- No clearly-visible weapon systems.
- LRLAP turrets fitted sequentially, forward of superstructure.
- Aft flight deck with enclosed hangar for up to 2 medium-lift helicopters.

Note: Zumwalt class' hull and superstructure design gives it stealth capability against radar detection.

SENSORS

Air/Surface search/Navigation/Fire Control: AN/SPY-3 multi-function DBR X/S-band.

Sonars: AN/SQQ-90 integrated undersea warfare system comprised of AN/SQS-60, AN/SQS-61 hull-mounted, AN/SQR-20 towed array.

AIR SUPPORT

Helicopters: 2 x SH-60 LAMPS or MH-60R Seahawk, 3 x MQ-8 Fire Scout UAV.

Luhai

Class: Luhai Type 051B (DDG)

Country of Origin: China	
Operators: China	

Active: 1

Name (Pennant Number): SHENZHEN (167)

SPECIFICATION

Displacement, tons: 6,000.

Length, feet (meters): 508'6" (155) oa.

Beam, feet (meters): 56'5" (17.2) oa.

Draft, feet (meters): 19'8" (6).

Speed, knots: 31.

Range, nautical miles: 14,000.

Complement: 250 (40 Officers, 210 Enlisted)

ARMAMENT

Missiles: A/S – 2 x rocket system; SSM – 16 x YJ-12; (32) cells H/AJK-16 VLS including SAM - HHQ-16.

Guns: 1 x dual Type 79A 100mm gun, 2 x H/PJ-11 CIWS

Torpedoes: 2 x 3 (6) torpedo tubes with Yu-7 torpedo.

Decoys: SR-210A EW jammer; PJ-46 Type 946 chaff/decoy rocket launchers.

SENSORS

RECOGNITION FEATURES

- Raised bow with maindeck running level to stern.
- 3.9-in twin gun turret in A position.
- ASROC missile launcher in B position.
- 2 CIWS mounted atop hangar superstructure.
- Triple torpedo tubes aft of forward funnel.
- Flight deck at stern level with maindeck.
- Rectangular bridge superstructure and helicopter hangar aft of midships with 2 funnels separated by pyramid mast and octuple missile launchers.
- Forward pyramidal mast mounted atop bridge superstructure with vertical lattice behind horizontal radar aerial.

Long range air search: Type 517H-1 Knife Rest 2-D.

Air search: Type 382 Sea Eagle 3-D.

Air/Surface search: Type 364 Seagull-C.

Navigation: RM-1290.

Fire control: Type 345 Front Dome (YJ-12), Type 347G Rice Bowl (CIWS).

Sonars: DUBV-23 hull-mounted active; towed array sonars.

AIR SUPPORT

Helicopters: 1 x Ka-28 Helix or 2 x Z-9C Haitun

Luhu

RECOGNITION FEATURES

- High bow with maindeck running to stern.
- 3.9-in gun mounted in A position after forecastle.
- Octuple missile launcher mounted in B position forward bridge superstructure.
- 2 CIWS mounted port and starboard of hangar superstructure.
- Lattice mainmast mounted after main superstructure.
- Single funnel midships topped with black wedge screen.
- Missile launcher mounted between funnel and enclosed secondary mast, another mounted after enclosed secondary mast.
- Curved vertical radar aerial mounted atop aft superstructure, forward of CIWS.
- Open quarter deck below flight deck at stern.

Note: Luhu DDGs have a single funnel and raised CIWS turrets forward of bridge, unlike Luhai DDG, which has 2 funnels and missile launchers instead of CIWS.

Class: Luhu Type 052 (DDG)

Country of Origin: China

Operators: China

Active: 2

Name (Pennant Number): HARBIN (112), QINGDAO (113)

SPECIFICATION

Displacement, tons: 6,100 , 4,600 full.

Length, feet (meters): 465'11" (142) oa.

Beam, feet (meters): 49'3" (15) oa.

Draft, feet (meters): 16'9" (5.1).

Speed, knots: 31.

Range, miles: 5,000 at 15 kts.

Complement: 260 (40 Officers and 220 Enlisted)

ARMAMENT

Missiles: A/S – 2 x 6 (12) Type 87 launchers; SAM – 1 x 8 (8) HHQ-7/CSA-N-4 + 16; SSM – 4 x 4 (16) YJ-83/CSS-N-8 Saccade.

Guns: 1 x 2 100mm H/PJ33B gun, 2 x 30mm Type 730 CIWS.

Torpedoes: 2 x 3 (6) Type 7424 324mm torpedo tubes with Yu-7 torpedo.

Decoys: Type 984 ECM, Type 928A ESM; 2 x Type 946 (15) chaff/decoy launcher.

SENSORS

Long range air search: Type 517M.

Air/surface search: Type 364.

Navigation: RM-1290.

Fire control: Type 344 for 100mm Type 79A; Type 345 for HHQ-7; Type 347G Rice Lamp for 37mm Type 76A.

Sonars: DUBV-23/SJD-7 (112) and DUBV-23/SJD-9 (113) hull-mounted, DUBV-43/ESS-1 towed array.

AIR SUPPORT

Helicopters: 2 x Ka-27 Helix or 2 x Z-9C Haitun.

Luyang I/II/III

Class: Luyang I/II/III Type 052B/C/D (DDG)

Country of Origin: China

Operators: China

Active: 35 (I) 2, (II) 6, (III) 25 + 2 fitting out

Building: 3

Planned: (III) 37

Name (Pennant Number): (I) GUANGZHOU (168), WUHAN (169), (II) LANZHOU (170), HAIKOU (171), CHANGCHUN (150), ZHENGZHOU (151), JINAN (152), XIAN (153), (III) XINING (117), URUMQI (118), GUIYANG (119), CHENGDU (120), QIQIHAR (121), TANGSHAN (122), HUAINAN (123), KAIFENG (124), TAIYUAN (131), SUZHOU (132), BAOTOU (133), SHAOXING (134), XIAMEN (154), NANJING (155), ZIBO (156), YEOSU (157), HOHHOT (161), NANNING (162), JIAOZUO (163), ZHANJIANG (165), GUILIN (164), KUNMING (172), CHANGSHA (173), HEFEI (174), YINCHUAN (175), ---, ---, ---, ----, ----

SPECIFICATION

Displacement, tons: (I) 6,500 full, (II) 7,000, (III) 7,500.

Length, feet (meters): (I/II) 509 (154), (III) 515 (157), (III 132, 162) 528'3"(161) oa.

Beam, feet (meters): 56 (17.2) oa.

Draft, feet (meters): 20 (6).

Speed, knots: 29.

Range, miles: 4,500 at 15 kts.

Complement: 280 (40 Officers, 240 Enlisted).

ARMAMENT

Missiles: SAM – (I) 2 x 24 (48) Shtil-1, (II) 6 x 8 (48) HHQ-9, (III) HHQ-10 CIWS; SSM – (I) 4 x 4 (16) YJ-83/CSS-N-8 Saccade; (II) 2 x 4 (8) YJ-62; (III) 2 x 32 (64) cell GJB 5860-2006 VLS with A/S – CY-5, SAM – HHQ-9, SSM – YJ-18/CH-SS-NX-13.

Guns: (I/II) 1 x 3.9-in/100mm H/PJ87 (III) 1 x 130mm H/PJ-38 gun, 2 x 30mm H/PJ12 Type 730 CIWS; (III 8th ship+) 1x 30mm H/PJ11.

Torpedoes: 2 x 3 (6) Type 7424 324mm tubes with Yu-7 torpedoes.

Decoys: (I) RJZ-726 ECM, (II) NRJ-6A ECM, (III) H/RJZ-726 ECM; 4 x 18 (72) H/RJZ-726 4A chaff/flare launcher.

RECOGNITION FEATURES

- Angled, high bow, with break between bow and forecastle.
- Gun turret in A position (I/II) 3.9-in/100mm, (III) 5.1-in/130mm.
- (I) CIWS mounted on sponsons port and starboard midships, (II/III) H/PJ12/11 CIWS mountings in B position and atop hangar superstructure - (III) HHQ-10 CIWS atop hangar superstructure.
- Aft flight deck, level with maindeck
- Forward mast atop bridge superstructure with vertical enclosed pylon supporting Type 364 air/surface search radar aerial.
- (III) 32-cell VLS batteries housed between A position 5.1-in/130mm gun and B position CIWS mounting, and aft of midships, forward of aft CIWS mounting.

Note: Luyang II and III bridge superstructure noticeably taller and bridge at higher elevation than Luyang I, Luyang II flight deck lower than maindeck.

Note: Luyang III is only variant with VLS cells.

SENSORS

Air search: (I) MAE-5 Fregat/Top Plate 3D; (II) H/JLG-346 AESA, Type 517; (III) H/JLG-346A Dragon Eye, H/LJQ-517/Knife Rest, H/LJQ-364 air-surface search.

Surface search: (II) Type 364 air-surface, Type 366; (III) H/LJQ-366 OTH.

Fire control: (I) Mineral-ME/Band Stand (YJ-83), MR-90 Front Dome, Type 344 (gun); (III) H/LJP-344A, H/LJP-349.

Sonars: (I/II) hull-mounted, towed array sonars; (III) H/SJD-9 hull-mounted, H/SJG-311 VDS towed array.

AIR SUPPORT

Helicopters: 1 x Ka-28 Helix or Z-9C Haitun.

Luzhou

Ministry of Defense of Japan Photo

Class: Luzhou Type 051C (DDG)

Country of Origin: China

Operators: China

Active: 2

Name (Pennant Number): SHENYANG (115), SHIJIAZHUANG (116).

SPECIFICATION

Displacement, tons: 7,100 full.

Length, feet (meters): 508'6" (155) oa.

Beam, feet (meters): 56 (17.2) oa.

Draft, feet (meters): 19'8" (6).

Speed, knots: 30.

Complement: 250.

ARMAMENT

Missiles: SSM – 2 x 4 (8) YJ-83/CSS-N-8 Saccade; 6 x 8 (48) VLS tubes supporting SAM – S-300FM/SA-N-20 Gargoyle.

Guns: 1 x 3.9-in/100mm Type 210 gun, 2 x 30mm H/PJ12 Type 730 CIWS.

Torpedoes: 2 x 3 (6) Type 7424 324mm tubes with Yu-7 torpedoes.

Decoys: 2 x 15 (30) Type 946 decoy launchers, 2 x 18 (36) Type 726 decoy launchers.

SENSORS

Long range air search: Mineral-ME/Band Stand OTH, MAE-5 Fregat/Top Plate PESA.

Air search: Type 364/SR-64 Seagull-C.

Surface search: MR-36/Type 362 air-surface search.

Fire control: 30-N-6 Tombstone, Type 347G (CIWS).

Sonars: hull-mounted, towed array sonars.

RECOGNITION FEATURES

- Sloped bow with continuous maindeck from bow to stern.
- Black-banded funnels located aft of bridge superstructure (slanted aft) and forward of aft superstructure (level top).
- Top Plate radar support atop enclosed aft mast, between superstructures.
- 3.9-in/100mm gun in A position.
- 2 x 8 VLS cells in B position, 4 x 8 VLS cells located in aft superstructure, forward of flight deck.
- Triple torpedo tubes located forward of midships, aft of bridge superstructure on port and starboard side.
- CIWS mounted on sponsons port and starboard midships.
- Quad missile launchers located aft of forward funnel, between torpedo tubes and CIWS sponsons.

Note: flight deck at stern supports 1 helicopter, but no hangar facility.

AIR SUPPORT

Helicopters: flight deck supports 1 x Ka-28 Helix or Z-9C Haitun.

Sovremenny

Class: Sovremenny Project 956 Sarych / Hangzhou Type 956 (DDG)

Country of Origin: Soviet Union	
Operators: Russia, China	
Active: 3 Russia, 2 China	

Name (Pennant Number): Russia – BURNY (778), NASTOYCHIVY (610), ADMIRAL USHAKOV (434); China – HANGZHOU (136), FUZHOU (137), TAIZHOU (138), NINGBO (139).

SPECIFICATION

Displacement, tons: 6,600 standard, 7,940 full.

Length, feet (meters): 511'10" (156) oa.

Beam, feet (meters): 56'9" (17.3) oa.

Draft, feet (meters): 21'4" (6.5).

Speed, knots: 32.

Range, miles: 4,000 at 18 kts.

Complement: 250 (40 Officers, 210 Enlisted).

ARMAMENT

Missiles: SAM- 2 x SA-N-12 Yezh/SA-N-12/17 Grizzly; SSM – 2 x quad (8) 3M-80E Moskit/SS-N-22 Sunburn.

Guns: 4 x 130mm/70 AK 130 (2 twin), 2 x 30mm CADS-N-1 Kashtan CIWS.

Torpedoes: 4 x 21-in/533mm 2 (twin) tubes.

Depth Charges: 2 x 6 (12) RBU 1000.

Mines: up to 40.

Decoys: 8 x PL 10, 2 x PL 2 (200) chaff launchers.

RECOGNITION FEATURES

- High bow with sweeping maindeck running aft to break at bridge superstructure, punctuated by quad missile launchers fitted port and starboard.
- 5.1-in guns mounted in A and Y positions.
- Missile launcher mounted in B position.
- Top Plate radar aerial fitted atop pyramidal mast, itself mounted on the aft end of the bridge superstructure.
- Single square funnel aft of midships.
- Lattice secondary mast fitted after funnel atop hangar superstructure.
- Raised flight deck in X position.
- Missile launcher mounted between flight deck and 5.1-in gun in Y position.

SENSORS

Air search: Top Plate 3D.

Surface search: Palm Frond.

Fire control: Front Dome (SA-N-7/17); Kite Screech (gun); Bass Tilt (CIWS).

Sonars: MGK-335 Platina/Bull Horn and Whale Tongue hull-mounted.

AIR SUPPORT

Helicopters: (Russia) 1 x Ka-27PL Helix (ASW); (China) 2 x Z-9 Haitun or Ka-28 Helix (ASW)

Udaloy I/II/III

Class: Udaloy I/II/III Project 1155 Fregat (DDG)

Country of Origin: Soviet Union

Operators: Russia

Active: 7 (I) 6, (II) 1

Name (Pennant Number): (I) ADMIRAL TRIBUTS (564), MARSHAL SHAPOSHNIKOV (543), SEVEROMORSK (619), ADMIRAL LEVCHENKO (605), ADMIRAL VINOGRADOV, ADMIRAL PANTELEYEV (648); (II) ADMIRAL CHABANENKO (650).

SPECIFICATION

Displacement, tons: 6,700 standard, 8,500 full (I); 7,700 standard, 8,900 full.

Length, feet (meters): 536'5" (163.5) oa.

Beam, feet (meters): 63'4" (19.3) oa.

Draft, feet (meters): 24'7" (7.5).

Speed, knots: (I) 29, (II) 28.

Range, miles: (I) 7,700 at 18 kts, (II) 4,000 at 18 kts.

Complement: 318 (37 Officers, 281 Enlisted)

ARMAMENT

Missiles: A/S – (I) 2 x 4 (8) SS-N-15 Silex with Type 53-72 torpedo or nuclear, (II) SS-N-15 Starfish with Type 40 torpedo,

; SAM – 8 x Klinok/SA-N-9 Gauntlet VLS, (II) 2 x SA-N-11 Grisson; (II) SSM – 2 x 4 (8) 3M-82 Moskit/SS-N-22 Sunburn.

Guns: (I) 2 x 3.9-in/100mm, 4 x 30mm/65 AK 630 CIWS' (II) 2 x 130mm/70 (twin) AK 130, 2 x CADS-N-1 Kashtan CIWS.

Torpedoes: 2x4 (8) 21-in/533mm tubes for (I) Type 53/65 torpedoes, (II) SS-N-16 Stallion A/S missiles.

Depth Charges: (I) 2 x 12 (24) RBU6000, (II) 2 x 10 (20) RBU12000.

Mines: (I) up to 26 mines.

Decoys: Bell Squat ECM; 2 x PK 2, 8 x PK 10 chaff launchers.

RECOGNITION FEATURES

- High bow with sweeping maindeck running aft to break after second funnel. (II) torpedo tubes fitted in hull above chine at break aft of second funnel.
- (I) 3.9-in guns mounted in A and B positions, (II/III) 3.9-in gun in A position.
- (II) Chaff launcher in B position, (III) VLS battery in B position.
- (All variants) VLS batteries fitted on forecastle and forward of helicopter hangar.
- 2 quad missile launchers fitted port and starboard of bridge superstructure.
- 2 pairs of square twin funnels with protruding screens aft.
- Pyramidal mast mounted on bridge superstructure.
- Lattice mast mounted atop bridge superstructure, after of pyramidal mast. Second and taller lattice mounted forward of second funnel.
- Crane fitted aft of second funnel.
- Hangar superstructure support two garages, forward of flight deck at stern.

SENSORS

Air search: MR-320M Topaz-V/Strut Pair, MR-760MA Fregat/Top Plate 3D.

Surface search: MR-212/201-1Nayada/Palm Frond.

Fire control: (I) Eye Bowl (A/S), MR-123 Bass Tilt (CIWS), (I/II) MR-360 Podkat/Cross Sword (SAM), Kite Screech (guns).

Sonars: Polinom/Horse Jaw hull-mounted, Horse Tail towed array.

AIR SUPPORT

Helicopters: 2 x Ka-27 Helix (ASW).

Frigates

Constellation

US Navy Photo

Class: Constellation (FFG)

Country of Origin: America

Operators: America

Building: 1

Planned: 20

Name (Pennant Number):
CONSTELLATION (62), CONGRESS (63),
CHESAPEAKE (64), LAFAYETTE (65), ----.

SPECIFICATION

Displacement, tons: 7,219.

Length, feet (meters): 496' (151.2) oa.

Beam, feet (meters): 65' (19.8) oa.

Draft, feet (meters): 26' (7.9).

Speed, knots: 26+.

Range, miles: 6,000 at 16 kts.

Complement: 200 (24 Officers, 176 Enlisted).

ARMAMENT

Missiles: (32) Mk 41 VLS for SAM – RIM-66
SM-2MR, RIM-162 ESSM, RIM-174 ERAM.
SSM – 4 x 4 (16) for RGM-184A NSM/JSM,
RGM-84 Harpoon. 1 x Mk 49 RIM-116 RAM
CIWS.

Guns: 1 x Mk 110 57mm gun.

Decoys: 2 x SLQ-32(V)6 SEWIP block 2; 4 x
Mk 53 Nulka decoy launchers.

RECOGNITION FEATURES

- Raised bow with level maindeck to break at superstructure.
- 57mm gun in A position, VLS cells fitted between 57mm gun turret and forward bridge superstructure.
- Single, aft-angled mast atop bridge superstructure.
- Funnels integrated into both bridge superstructure aft of mast and aft superstructure, forward of helicopter hangar.
- Lifeboats on port and starboard slipways, aft of midships.
- CIWS mounted atop helicopter hangar on aft superstructure.

Note: Ship class design derived from French/Italian FREMM multipurpose frigate.

SENSORS
Air search: AN/SPY-6(V)3 EASR.

Surface search: AN/SPS-73(V)18.

Fire control:

Sonars: AN/SQS-62 variable-depth hull-mounted, AN/SLQ-61 towed array.

AIR SUPPORT
Helicopters: 1 x MH-60R Seahawk, 1 x MQ-8B/C Fire Scout UAV.

Freedom

Class: Freedom (LCS)

US Navy Photo

Country of Origin: America	
Operators: America	

Active: 8

Building: 3

Retired: 5

Name (Pennant Number): FORT WORTH (3), MILWAUKEE (5), DETROIT (7), LITTLE ROCK (9), SIOUX CITY (11), WICHITA (13), BILLINGS (15), INDIANAPOLIS (17), ST. LOUIS (19), MINNEAPOLIS-SAINT PAUL (21), COOPERSTOWN (23), MARINETTE (25), NANTUCKET (27), BELOIT (29), CLEVELAND (31).

SPECIFICATION

Displacement, tons: 3,900.

Length, feet (meters): 378 (115) oa.

Beam, feet (meters): 57'5" (17.5) oa.

Draft, feet (meters): 12'10" (3.9).

Ranges, miles: 3,500 at 18 kts.

Speed, knots: 47.

Complement: 50 (accommodation for 75).

ARMAMENT

Varies by mission module

Missiles: (1-15) 1 x Mk 49 missile launcher for SAM – RIM-116 RAM. May include (32) VLS cells for SAM - RIM-152 ESSM; 2 x 4 (8) RGM-184A NSM/JSM.

Guns: 1 x 57mm Mk 110 gun, 2 x .50cal MG. May include Mk 46 30mm gun system. (17-31) Mk 15 SeaRAM CIWS.

Decoys: WBR-2000 ESM, A/S SKWS decoy system.

RECOGNITION FEATURES

- Continuous, level deck from bow to stern, with vertically-angled slope to forward edge of bridge superstructure.
- 57mm gun in A position, forward of bridge superstructure.
- Single mast atop bridge superstructure.
- Two sets of twin funnels enclosed in bridge superstructure, aft of mast.
- Lifeboats sited on slipways midships on port and starboard.
- Flight deck comprises aft quarter of maindeck.
- CIWS mounted atop hangar forward of flight deck, in aft part of superstructure.

Note: Stern opening has capacity for 36-foot/11m RHIB high-speed boat.

SENSORS

Air/surface search: (1-15) AN/TRS-3D, (17+) AN/TRS-4D

Navigation/Fire control: COMBATSS-21 combat management system.

Sonars: (ASW mission module) AN/SQR-20 towed array.

AIR SUPPORT

Helicopters: 1 x MH-60R/S Seahawk, 1-2 x MQ-8B/MQ-8C Fire Scout UAV.

Independence

US Navy Photo

Class: Independence (LCS)

Country of Origin: America

Operators: America

Active: 14

Building: 2

Retired: 2

Name (Pennant Number): CORONADO (4), JACKSON (6), MONTEGOMERY (8), GABRIELLE GIFFORDS (10), OMAHA (12) MANCHESTER (14), TULSA (16), CHARLESTON (18), KANSAS CITY (22), OAKLAND (24), MOBILE (26), SAVANNAH (28), CANBERRA (30), SANTA BARBARA (32), AUGUSTSA (34), KINGSVILLE (36), PIERRE (38).

SPECIFICATION

Displacement, tons: 3,100

Length, feet (meters): 418 (127.4) oa.

Beam, feet (meters): 104 (31.6) oa.

Draft, feet (meters): 14 (4.3).

Speed, knots: 44+.

Range, miles: 4,300 at 18 kts.

Complement: 40 (accommodation for 75).

ARMAMENT

Varies by mission module

Missiles: 1 x Mk 15 SeaRAM CIWS. (Modular) (32) VLS cells to including SAM – RIM-162 ESSM; SSM - (8) RGM-84 Harpoon, (8) RGM-184A NSM, (24) AGM-114 LHM.

Guns: 1 x Mk 110 57mm gun, 4 x .50cal. MG; (Modular) Mk 46 30mm Bushmaster gun.

RECOGNITION FEATURES

- Trimaran hull with sloped sides on port and starboard.
- Single anchor mounted on bow.
- Tripod mast atop bridge superstructure supports radome aerial.
- Lifeboats on port and starboard slipways, forward of stern.
- 57mm gun in A position, missile launchers mounted forward of bridge superstructure.
- CIWS mounted in Y position atop aft end of bridge superstructure.
- Flight deck comprises approximate aft third of hull.

Decoys: ES-3601 ESM, 4 x SRBOC decoy launchers for chaff and IR decoys. Nuka active radar decoy system.

SENSORS

Air/surface search: AN/SPS-77(V)1 Sea Giraffe 3D.

Navigation: BridgeMaster E.

Fire control: ICMS, AN/KX-1 EO/IR.

Sonars: (MCM module) AN/AQS-20.

AIR SUPPORT

Helicopters: 1 x MH-60R/S Seahawk, 2 x MQ-8B/C Fire Scout.

Jiangkai I/II

Class: Jiangkai I/II Type 054/A (FFG)

Country of Origin: China

Operators: China

Active: 42 (054) 2 (054A) 40

Planned: (054) 2 (054A) 50

Name (Pennant Number): MAANSHAN (525), WENZHOU (526); (054A) XIANNING (500), BINZHOU (515), JIUJIANG (516), NANPING (517), ZIYANG (522), HEBI (523), ZHOUSHAN (529), XUZHOU (530), XIANGTAN (531), JINGZHOU (532), XUCHANG (536), ANQING (537), YANTAI (538), WUHU (539), XICHANG (540), ZHAOZHUANG (542), YANCHENG (546), LINYI (547), YIYANG (548), CHANGZHOU (549), WEIFANG (550), MAOMING (551), YIBIN (552), ZHAOTONG (555), YINGTAN (556), HENGYANG (568), YULIN (569), HUANGSHAN (570), YUNCHENG (571), HENGSHUI (572), LIUZHOU (573), SANYA (574), YUEYANG (575), DAQING (576), HUANGGANG (577), YANGZHOU (578), HANDAN (579), RIZHAO (59), ANYANG (599), NANTONG (601).

SPECIFICATION

Displacement, tons: 4,053.

Length, feet (meters): 440 (134.1) oa.

Beam, feet (meters): 52'6" (16) oa.

Draft, feet (meters): 16'5" (5).

Speed, knots: 27.

Range, miles: 8,025.

Complement: 165.

ARMAMENT

Missiles: A/S – 2 x 6 (36 missiles) Type 87 240mm ASROC, SSM - 2 x 4 (8) YJ-83/CSS-N-8 Saccade; (054) SAM - 1 x 8 (8) HQ-7; (054A) (32) VLS including A/S – Yu-8 ASROC, SAM – HQ-16..

Guns: (054) Type 210 100mm gun, (054A) 1 x PJ26 76mm gun; (054) 4 x AK 630 CIWS, (054A) 2 x Type 730 CIWS.

RECOGNITION FEATURES

- Sloped hull defined by high bow, raised gunwales for forecastle; and maindeck that runs without break to stern.
- Enclosed mast atop aft edge of bridge superstructure.
- Black-tipped funnel fitted aft of midships, on forward edge of aft superstructure.
- Main gun mounted in A position.
- SSM Saccade missile launchers mounted between bridge and aft superstructures.
- (054A) VLS cells fitted forward of bridge superstructure.

Note: Similar in appearance to France's La Fayette class frigate.

Torpedoes: 2 x 3 (6) 324mm tubes for Yu-7 torpedo.

Decoys: Type 922-1 RWR, HZ-100 ECM, Kashtan-3 missile jamming system; 2 x 18 (36) Type 726-4 decoy launchers.

SENSORS

Air search: (054) Type 363S Sea Tiger; (054A) Type 382/M2EM Top Plate, SR2410c AESA, Type 517, Type 344/MR331 Band Stand.

Surface search: Type 363S Sea Tiger, Type 362/MR-36A.

Navigation: Racal RM-1290.

Fire control: (054) Type 347G Rice Lamp, MR34 (gun), Type 345/MR-90/Front Dome

Sonars: (active-passive) H/SJD-307/MGK-335 hull-mounted; H/SJG-206 towed array.

AIR SUPPORT

Helicopters: 1 x Ka-28 Helix or Z-9C. Haitun

Jianghu II/V

Class: Jianghu II/V Type 053H1(II), 053H1G(V) (FFG)

Country of Origin: China

Operators: China

Active: 3, (II) 1, (V) 2.

Name (Pennant Number): (II) SHAOGUAN (553), (V) BEIHAI (558), FOSHAN (559).

SPECIFICATION
Displacement, tons: 1,457 standard, 1,702 full.

Length, feet (meters): 338'8" (103.2) oa.

Beam, feet (meters): 35'5" (10.8) oa.

Draft, feet (meters): 10 (3.1).

Speed, knots: 26.

Complement: 200.

ARMAMENT
Missiles: A/S – 2 x 6 (12) Type 3200 launcher ASROC, SSM - 2 x 4 (8) YJ-83/CSS-N-8 Saccade.

Guns: 2 x PJ33A 3.9-in/100mm gun, 4 x Type 76 (twin) 37mm CIWS.

Depth charges: 4 x depth charge projects, 2 x depth charge racks.

Decoys: RW-8 Jug Pair ECM/EW system.

SENSORS
Air search: Type 354 Eye Shield, Type 360S, Type 517.

Surface search: H/LJQ352/Type 352 Square Tie/Fin Curve.

Navigation: Racal RM-1290, Type 651A IFF.

RECOGNITION FEATURES
- High bow with maindeck running level to stern, low in water, (II) with hangar superstructure aft of funnel, forward flight deck. (V) maindeck elevated amidships.
- 3.9-in single or twin gun mounted in A position
- Lattice mainmast fitted after bridge superstructure. Secondary lattice mast with x-shaped aerial mounted on secondary superstructure after missile launchers, before 3.9in sun in Y position.
- Round, aft-angled funnel sited aft of midships, between missile launchers.
- (V) missile launchers mounted in pairs, trained outboard port and starboard, forward and aft of funnel.
- 2 CIWS mounted forward of bridge, some mounted additional 2 CIWS outboard of mainmast, other atop aft superstructure in X position.
- (II) 3.9-in gun in Y position and CIWS in X position replaced by helicopter hangar and flight deck, respectively, CIWS mounted aft of funnel.

Fire control: Type 341 (CIWS), Type 343G (gun/missile).

Sonars: SJD-5 MF hull-mounted (developed from MG-11/Stag Hoof), SJC-1B reconnaissance, SJX-4 communications.

AIR SUPPORT
Helicopters: 1 x Z-9C Haitun.

Jiangwei II

Class: Jiangwei II Type 053H2G (FFG)

Country of Origin: China

Operators: China

Active: 8

Name (Pennant Number): JIAXING (521),
YICHANG (564), HULUDAO (565),
SANMING (524), XIANGYANG (567),
HUAIHUA (566), LUOYANG (527),
MIANYANG (528).

SPECIFICATION

Displacement, tons: 2,250 standard, 2,393 full.

Length, feet (meters): 367'5" (112) oa.

Beam, feet (meters): 40'8" (12.4) oa.

Draft, feet (meters): 14'1" (4.3).

Speed, knots: 28.

Range, miles: 4,000 at 16 kts.

Complement: 168 (30 Officers, 138 Enlisted).

ARMAMENT

Missiles: SAM – 1 x 6 HQ-7, SSM - 2 x 4 (8)
YJ-83/CSS-N-18 Saccade.

Guns: 1 x PJ33A (twin) 3.9-in/100mm gun, 4 x
Type 76A (twin) 37mm CIWS.

Depth charges: 2 x Type 3100 racks and
launchers.

Torpedoes: 2 x 3 torpedo launchers.

Decoys: 2 x 15 (30) Type 946/PJ-46 decoy
launchers, RW-8 Jug Pair ECM/EW system,
Type 981-3 EW jammer, R-210 RW receiver,
Type 651A IFF.

SENSORS

Ministry of Defense of Japan Photo

RECOGNITION FEATURES

- High bow, with level maindeck
  running to flight deck at stern.
  Stepped superstructure with open
  quarterdeck below flight deck at
  stern.
- 2 CIWS mounted port and starboard,
  outboard forward of bridge
  superstructure.
- Lattice mainmast mounted at aft end
  of bridge superstructure.
- Single funnel with aft-protruding
  black screen aft of bridge, after
  midships.
- Missile launchers mounted before
  and after funnel.
- Boats in davits, port and starboard of
  funnel.
- CIWS mounted on sponsons atop
  hangar superstructure, forward of
  flight deck.

Air search: Type 517H-1 Knife Rest.

Air/Surface search: Type 360.

Navigation: RM-1290.

Fire control: Type 343G (gun, SSM), Type
345/MR35 (SAM), Type 347G Rice Lamp
(CIWS).

Sonars: SJD-5 MF hull-mounted (developed
from MG-11/Stag Hoof).

AIR SUPPORT

Helicopters: 1 x Z-9C Haitun

Admiral Gorshkov

Class: Admiral Gorshkov Project 22350 (FFG)

Ministry of Defense of Russia Photo

Country of Origin: Russia

Operators: Russia

Active: 2 + 1 in sea trials

Building: 5

Planned: 15

Name (Pennant Number): ADMIRAL FLOTA
SOVETSKOGO SOYUZA GORSHKOV (921),
ADMIRAL FLOTA KASATONOV (922),
ADMIRAL GOLOVKO (923), ADMIRAL
FLOTA SOVETSKOGO SOYUZA ISAKOV
(924), ADMIRAL AMELKO (925), ADMIRAL
CHICHAGOV (926), ADMIRAL YUMASHEV
(927), ADMIRAL SPIRIDONOV (928).

SPECIFICATION
Displacement, tons: 4,500 standard, 5,400 full.

Length, feet (meters): 443 (135) oa.

Beam, feet (meters): 52'6" (16) oa.

Draft, feet (meters): 14'9" (4.5).

Speed, knots: 29.

Ranges, miles: 4,500.

Complement: 170.

ARMAMENT
Missiles: SAM - 4 x 8 (32) 9M96/S-400 SA-21
Growler; 2 x 8 (16) (925+) 3 x 8 (24) VLS cells
for A/S – 91RT Otvet/Club-N, SSM - 3K55
Oniks/SS-N-26 Strobile, 3M14K Kalibr/SS-N-
27 Sizzler, 3K22 Zirkon/SS-N-33.

Guns: 1 – 130mm A-192 Armat gun, 2 x 6
30mm 3M89 Palash CIWS, 2 x 14.5mm MTPU-
1 MG

Torpedoes: 2 x 4 (8) 13-in/330mm torpedo
tubes for MMT torpedoes, M-15 anti-torpedoes.

RECOGNITION FEATURES
- Level bow with maindeck running
  level from bow to break at flight
  deck.
- 5.1-in gun mounted in A position,
  VLS cells sited forward of bridge
  superstructure.
- Lifeboats sited in port and starboard
  slipways aft of forecastle, forward of
  VLS cells.
- Enclosed aerial radome mounted
  atop bridge.
- Pyramidal, enclosed mast fitted at aft
  end of bridge superstructure.
- Single funnel fitted aft of bridge,
  after midships.
- Hangar superstructure mounted after
  funnel, forward flight deck.

Decoys: 4 x KT-308 decoy launchers, 8 x KT-
216 launchers (Prosvet-M), TK-28 ESM, 5P42
Filin jammer, MDM-2 deflection system.

SENSORS
Air search: 5P-27 Furke, 5P-20K Poliment
4AESA.

Surface search: 34K1 Monolit.

Navigation: MR-231 Nayada.

Fire control: 3R14N, 5P-20K Poliment, 5P-10
Puma.

Sonars: Zarya 3.3 hull-mounted, Vinyetka towed
array.

AIR SUPPORT
Helicopters: 1 x Ka-27 Helix

Gepard

Class: Gepard Project 11661 (FFG)

Country of Origin: Russia

Operators: Russia

Active: 2

Name (Pennant Number): TATARSTAN (691), DAGESTAN (693).

SPECIFICATION

Displacement, tons: 1,500 standard, 1,805 full.

Length, feet (meters): 335 (102.1) oa.

Beam, feet (meters): 43'4" (13.2) oa.

Draft, feet (meters): 11'6" (3.5).

Speed, knots: 28.

Range, miles: 5,000 at 10 kts, 3,800 at 14 kts, 1,750 at 22 kts, 950 at 27 kts.

Complement: 121 (15 Officers, 106 Enlisted).

ARMAMENT

Missiles: SSM - 2 x 4 (8) 3K24 Uran launchers for 3M24 Zvezda/AS-20 Kayak, (8) VLS cells for SSM – 3M14K Kalibr/SS-N-27 Sizzler. (691) SAM – (20) 9M33 Osa/SA-N-4 Gecko.

Guns: 1 x 76mm AK-176 gun, (691) 2x 30mm AK-630M CIWS, (693) 1 x 30mm Palash CIWS, 2 x 14.5mm MTPU MG

Torpedoes: 4 x 21-in/533mm tubes.

Mines: 20.

Wikimedia Commons Photo

RECOGNITION FEATURES

- High bow with continuous maindeck running from bow to stern.
- 5.1-in gun mounted in A position.
- Lifeboats sited amidships, port and starboard of superstructure.
- Bridge sited slightly forward of midships.
- Single, enclosed mast aft of bridge and radome atop superstructure.
- Single, large funnel amidships, separate and aft of bridge superstructure.

Note: No flight deck or helicopter hangar.

Decoys: TK-25 ESM, 4 x KT-216 launchers for PK-10 decoys, AZ-SO/SR/SOM/SK/SMZ-50 rounds.

SENSORS

Air/surface search: 34K1 Monolit radar complex, MR-352 Pozitiv, (693) ME-1 Pozitiv.

Navigation: MR-212 Vaygach, (691) MR-5PV Gals.

Fire control: MR-123 Vympel-A (gun, 3RP14N (Kalibr).

Sonars: (691) MG-757 Anapa-M hull-mounted, (693) Zarnitsa hull-mounted

Krivak I/II/IV

Class: Krivak I/II/IV Project 1135 Burevestnik (FF)

George Chernilevsky Photo

Country of Origin: Soviet Union/Russia

Operators: Russia

Active: 5 (I) 1, (II) 1, (IV) 3

Building: 1 (IV)

Name (Pennant Number): (I) LADNY (16), (II) PYTLIVY (169), (IV) ADMIRAL GRIGOROVICH, (1357)) ADMIRAL ESSEN (1358), ADMIRAL MAKAROV (1359), ADMIRAL KORNILOV (1362).

SPECIFICATION

Displacement, tons: (I) 2,835 standard, 3,190 full, (II) 2,935 standard, 3,190 full, (IV) 3,350 standard, 3,860 full.

Length, feet (meters): 403'6" (123), (IV) 409'5" (124.8) oa.

Beam, feet (meters): 46'7" (14.2), (IV) 49' 10"(15.2) oa.

Draft, feet(meters):(I-II)14'9"(4.5),(IV)15'5" (4.7)

Speed, knots: (I, II, IV) 30.

Range, miles: (I-II) 4,000, (IV) 4,850 at 14 kts.

Complement: (I-II) 192 (23 Officers, 169 Enlisted), (IV) 220.

ARMAMENT

Missiles: A/S - (I-II) 1 x (4) KT-M-1135 URK-5 Rastrub-B launchers for 85RU ASROC, (IV) (IV) 1 x 12 RBU-6000 RPL-8 launcher for (48) RGB-60 or 90R ASROC; SAM - (I-II) 4 x 10 (40) (IV) 8 x (8) Igla-1E/SA-N-18 Grouse; SAM – 2 x 12 (24) VLS cells for 9M317E Buk/SA-N-12 Grizzly, SSM – (8) 3S14E VLS cells for 3M54T or 3M14T Kalibr/SS-N-27 Sizzler.

Guns: (I-II) 2 x (twin) 76mm AK-726 gun, (IV) 1 3.9-in/100mm A-190-01 gun, 2 x Kashtan CIWS/CADS-N-1 (30mm (12)/32 (64) 9M311E/SA-N-11 Grison), 2 x 12.7 mm 6P58 MG.

Depth Charges: (IV) 2 x 10 (20) 55mm DP-65 grenade launcher for RG-55M, GRS-55 grenades.

Torpedoes: 2 x 4 (8) (IV) 2 x 2 (4) 21-in/533mm torpedo tubes for SET-65, 5365K torpedoes.

Mines: (I-II) 4-18 mines (PMR-1/2, MTPK-1, RM-1, UDM-2, KSM, KAM, KB Krab, Serpey, UDM-2, IGDM-500)

Mortars: (I-II) 2 x 12 (24) RBU-6000 Smerch-2

Decoys: MP-401S Start-S ESM Radar system, (I-II) 4 x KL-101 launchers for PK-16 decoy, Nickel-KM IFF, (IV) 4 x KT-216 launchers for PK-10 decoys.

SENSORS

Air/surface search radar: MR-310 Angara-A/Head Net, (203, IV) MR-750 Fregat-M2/Top Plate.

Surface Search: (IV) TK-25

Fire Control: MR-114 Lev (gun), Burya (mortars), MR-123 Vympel (CIWS), (I-II) ARP-50R radio direction finder, SU-85KS-I Musson-U (ASROC), (IV) 5P-10E Puma (gun), 3R91E1 (SAM), 3R-14N-11356 (SSM), 3TS-25EK target designation.

Navigation: MR-212/201 Vaygach-U navigation/Palm Frond, (I-II) MR-220 Reyd/Peel Cone, (IV) Bridge-Master.

Sonar: (hull-mounted) (I-II) MG-332 Titan-2/Bull Nose, MG-325 Vega/Mare Tail, MGS-400K, MG-7 Braslet anti-saboteur, KMG-12 Kassandra, MI-110R & MI-110K/M wake detectors, (IV) MGK-335MS Platina-MS/Mare Tail; MG-757.1 Anapa-M anti-saboteur.

AIR SUPPORT

Helicopters: (I-II) 1 Ka-27PS Helix, (IV) 1 x Ka-28 Helix (ASW) or Ka-31 Helix (AEW), 1 x Ortlan-10 UAV.

Neustrashimiy

Class: Neustrashimiy Project 11540 Yastreb (FF)

Country of Origin: Soviet Union

Operators: Russia

Active: 2

Name (Pennant Number): NEUSTRASHIMY (401), YAROSLAV MUDRY (402).

SPECIFICATION

Displacement, tons: 3,950 standard, 4,350 full.

Length, feet (meters): 425'10" (129.8) oa.

Beam, feet (meters): 51'2" (15.6) oa.

Draft, feet (meters): 15'9" (4.8).

Speed, knots: 29.

Complement: 210 (35 Officers, 175 Enlisted).

ARMAMENT

Missiles: A/S – 6 x URPK-6 Vodopad for 83R/84R ASROC, 4 x 12 (48) RBU-6000 RPK-8 launchers for RGB-60 or 90R ASROC, SAM – 4 x 8 (32) 9M330 Kinzhal/SA-N-9 Gauntlet, (402) SSM – 2 x 4 (8) 3M24 Uran/SS-N-25 Switchblade.

Guns: 1 x 3.9-in/100mm AK-100 gun, 2 x 3M87 Kortik 30mm/2 x 4 (8) SAM) CIWS, 1 x 45mm/68 21-KM AAA, (402) 2 x 12.7 mm NSVT MG.

Depth Charges: (402) 2 x 10 (20) 55mm DP-65 grenade launchers for RG-55M, GRS-55 grenades.

Mines: 16-20.

Decoys: MP-405 ESM, 2 x KL-101 for PL-16 decoys, 8 x KT-216 launchers for PL-10 decoys.

US Navy Photo

RECOGNITION FEATURES

- High bow with continuous maindeck running from bow to flight deck above quarterdeck.

- 3.9-in gun mounted in A position, depth charge launcher mounted in B position, VLS cell battery fitted between A and B positions.

- Forward, secondary mast fitted atop bridge superstructure, forward twin funnels fitted aft of bridge superstructure.

- Pyramidal mainmast fitted atop aft superstructure to support Top Plate radar aerial.

- 2 horizontal torpedo launchers mounted port and starboard alongside aft funnel fitted into aft superstructure.

- CIWS mounted at aft end of aft superstructure forward of flight deck.

Note: Aft funnel is flush to maindeck, not visible in profile.

SENSORS

Air/surface search: MR-750 Fregat-M2/Top Plate.

Navigation: MR-212 Vaygach/Palm Frond.

Fire control: Onega-11540 (A/S), K-12/Cross Sword (SAM), MR-145 Lev-218 (gun),

Sonars: MGK-365 Zvezda-M1 hull-mounted, (401) Zarya-SK hull-mounted.

AIR SUPPORT

Helicopters: 1 Ka-27 Helix.

Corvettes

Jiangdao II

Ministry of Defense of Japan Photo

Class: Jiangdao II Type 056A (FFL)

Country of Origin: China	
Operators: China	

Active: 50

Name (Pennant Number): HUANGSHI (502), SUQIAN (504), QINHUANGDAO (505), JINGMEN (506), TONGREN (507), QUJING (508), EZHOU (513), LIUPANSHUI (514), YIWU (518), HANZHONG (520), XUANCHENG (535), WUHAI (540), ZHANGYE (541), SUINING (551), GUANGYAN (552), DEYANG (554), YICHUN (556), NANCHONG (557), SANMENXIA (593), ZHUZHOU (594), MATSUBARA (600), PINGDINGSHAN (602), GINZHOU (603), MUDANJIANG (604), ZHANGJIAKOU (605), DONGYING (606), LAIWU (607), LIAOCHENG (608), SHIZUISHAN (609), SHUOZHOU (610), LU'AN (611), XIAOGAN (615), TAI'AN (616), JINGDEZHEN (617), SHANGQIU (618), NANYANG (619), GANZHOU (620), PANZHIHUA (621), GUANG'AN (622), WENSHAN (623), SUIZHOU (624), BAZHONG (625), WUZHOU (626), ENSHI (627), YONGZHOU (628), TONGLING (629), ABA (630), TIANMEN (631), JINING (636), SHIYAN (637).

SPECIFICATION

Displacement, tons: 1,300 standard, 1,500 full.

Length, feet (meters): 292 (88.9) oa.

Beam, feet (meters): 26'5" (11.14) oa.

Draft, feet (meters): 13'2" (4).

Speed, knots: 30.

Range, miles: 3,500 at 16 kts, 2,000 at 18 kts.

Complement: 78.

ARMAMENT

Missiles: SAM – 1 x 8 HHQ-10 CIWS; SSM – 2 x 2 (4) YJ-83/CSS-N-8 Saccade.

Guns: 1 x 3-in/76mm H/PJ-26 gun, 2 x 30mm H/PJ-17 CIWS,

RECOGNITION FEATURES

- High bow with maindeck break at superstructure, elevated flight deck without hangar above semi-open quarterdeck.
- Superstructure sides sheer with hull.
- 3-in gun mounted in A position.
- Torpedo tubes angled outboard, port and starboard, fitted between bridge superstructure and funnel.
- Single black-tipped funnel fitted amidships, between bridge and aft superstructures.
- CIWS missile launcher mounted on aft superstructure forward of flight deck

Note: Equipped with towed passive sonar array and hull-mounted, active VDS.

Torpedoes: 2 x 3 (6) 12.8-in/324mm tubes for Yu-7 torpedoes.

Decoys: ECM suite, 2 x 5 (10) decoy launchers.

SENSORS

Air/surface search: Type 360S Seagull.

Air traffic control: Type 754 helicopter control and approach.

Navigation: Type 760.

Fire control: Type LR-66, Type 347G

Sonars: hull-mounted VDS, towed array.

AIR SUPPORT

Helicopters: able to land, but not to store 1 x Z-9C Haitun.

Dergach

Class: Dergach Project 1239 Sivuch (FFLG)

Country of Origin: Soviet Union

Operators: Russia

Active: 2

Name (Pennant Number): BORA (616), SAMUM (615).

SPECIFICATION

Displacement, tons: 897 standard, 1,083 full.

Length, feet (meters): 209'8" (63.9) oa.

Beam, feet (meters): 56'5" (17.2) oa.

Draft, feet (meters): 11'10" (3.6).

Speed, knots: 52.

Range, miles: 2,500 at 12 kts, 800 at 45 kts.

Complement: 68 (9 Officers, 59 Enlisted).

ARMAMENT

Missiles: SAM – 2 x 10 (20) 4K22AM Osa-MA2 for 9MM33,9M33M,9M33M1,9M33M5/SA-N-4 Gecko, 2 x 9K34 Strela-3 for (8) 9M36 ; SSM – 2 x 2 (4) YJ-83/CSS-N-8 Saccade; SSM – 2 x 4 (8) 3M80 Moskit/SS-N-22 Sunburn.

Guns: 1 x 3-in/76mm AK-176M gun, 2 x 30mm AK-630M CIWS,

RECOGNITION FEATURES

- Distinctive catamaran hull, with level maindeck from bow to stern.
- Singular superstructure supports Monolit radar aerial atop bridge, two enclosed mainmasts, ends at stern.
- Quadruple SSM launchers mounted port and starboard alongside superstructure
- 3-in gun mounted in A position, CIWS in B position, additional CIWS mounted atop aft end of superstructure at stern.
- Missile launcher mounted forward of aft CIWS, atop superstructure.

Note: Dergach design is distinct for catamaran hull and superstructure that ends at stern.

Decoys: Vympel-R2 ESM suite, MP-405-1 ESM system; 2 x KL-101 launchers for PK-16, 4 x KT-216 launchers for PK-10.

SENSORS

Air/surface search: 34K1 Monolit complex (most, Mayak, Mech, Massiv, MR-144), MR-352 Pozitiv-ME1/Cross Round.

Navigation: MR-231-1, Don.

Fire control: 4R-33AM (SSM), Pop group (SAM), MR-123-01 Vympel-A/Bass Tilt (gun

Gremyashchiy

Class: Gremyashchiy Project 20385 (FFL)

Country of Origin: Russia

Operators: Russia

Active: 1

Building: 4, 6 planned

Name (Pennant Number): GREMYASHCHIY
(337), PROVORNIY, BUYNIY, RAZUMNIY,
BYSTRIY, RETIVIY.

SPECIFICATION
Displacement, tons: 1800 standard, 2500 full.

Length, feet (meters): 344'6" (106) oa.

Beam, feet (meters): 42'8" (13) oa.

Draft, feet (meters): 17'11" (5.45).

Speed, knots: 27.

Range, miles: 4,000 at 14 kts.

Complement: 99 (14 Officers, 85 Enlisted).

ARMAMENT
Missiles: 1 x 8 (8) UKSK VLS battery
supporting Kalibr missile family, including A/S
– 91RT Otvet/Club-N; SSM - 3K55 Oniks/SS-
N-26 Strobile, 3M14K Kalibr/SS-N-27 Sizzler,
3K22 Zirkon/SS-N-33. SAM – 3 x 4 (12) 3K96
Redut cells for 32 9M96/SA-21 Growler or 48
9M100 Vityaz/SA-10 Grumble, 1 x 8 3M87
launcher for (64) 9M311 (CIWS).

Guns: 1 x 3.9-in/100mm A-190 gun, 2 x 30mm
AK-630M CIWS. 2 x 14.5mm MTPU-1 Zhalo.

Torpedoes: 2 x 4 (8) 12.75-in/324mm SM-588
Paket NK launchers for 8 MTT torpedoes, M-15
anti-torpedoes.

Ministry of Defense of Russia Photo

RECOGNITION FEATURES
- Raised bow with maindeck running from bow to flight deck at stern.
- Superstructure sides are sheer to hull, port and starboard.
- Enclosed mast radome aerial aft of bridge atop superstructure.
- VLS battery fitted aft of turret in A position, forward bridge superstructure.
- Black-tipped funnel centered midships.

Note: Similar design characteristics to Steregushchiy (Project 20380), which Gremyashichiy-class follows.

Depth Charges: 2 x 2 (4) 45mm DP-64
launchers.

Decoys: TK-25-2 ESM, 4 x KT-216 PK-10
decoy launchers.

SENSORS
Air search: 5P-20K-A Monument-A, 5P-27M
Furke-2, Sandal-V, Parol IFF.

Navigation: MR-231, MR-231-2, PAL-N.

Fire control: 5P-10-02 Puma-02 (gun), MR-123-
02 Sfera (CIWS), 3R14N (Kalibr).

Sonars: Zarya-2, Minotavr-ISPN-M, Anapa
GISZ, Anapa-M anti-saboteur.

AIR SUPPORT
Helicopter: 1 x Ka-27 Helix

Grisha I/III

Class: Grisha Project 1124/M Albatros (FFL)

US Navy Photo

Country of Origin: Soviet Union

Operators: Russia

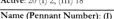

Active: 20 (I) 2, (III) 18

Name (Pennant Number): (I)
ALEKSANDROVETS (059), KHOLMSK (369); **(III)**
POVORINO (053), YEYSK (054), KASIMOV (055),
MUROMETS (064), SUZDALETS (071), YUNGA
(113), NARYAN-MAR 138), ONEGA (164), BREST
(199), MONCHEGORSK (190), SNEZHNOGORSK
(196), METEL (323), MPK-107 (332), SOVYETSKAYA
GAVAN' (350), MPK-221 (354), UST-ILIMSK (362),
MPK-82 (375), KORYEYETS (390).

SPECIFICATION

Displacement, tons: (I) 835 standard, 990 full;

(III) 910 standard, 1,055 full.

Length, feet (meters): 233 (71.1) oa.

Beam, feet (meters): 33'6" (10.2) oa.

Draft, feet (meters): (I) 11'6" (3.5); (III) 12'2"

(3.7).

Speed, knots: (I) 36), (III) 32.

Range, miles: 4,000 at 10 kts, 2,700 at 14 kts.

Complement: (I) 83 (9 Officers, 74 Enlisted), (III)

90.

ARMAMENT

Missiles: A/S – 2 x 12 RBU-6000 Smerch

launchers for (96) RGB-60; SAM – 1 x 2 ZIF-22

Osa-M launchers for (20) 9M33/SA-N-4a Gecko,

(II) 4 x 9K34 Strela-3 for (8) 9M36/SA-N-8

Gremlin or 9M39/SA-N-10 Grouse.

Guns: (I) 2 x 57mm AK-725 or 30mm AK-630

CIWS; (II) 1 x 3-in/76mm AK-176 gun, 1 x 30mm

AK-630M CIWS.

Torpedoes: 2 x 2 (4) 21-in/533mm DTA-53-1124

tubes.

Depth charges: 12 BB-1 or BPS.

Mines: 18

Decoys: (II) 2 x KL-101 for PK-16, 4 KT-216 for

PK-10.

SENSORS

Air search: (I) MR-302 Rubka (MPK-8, MR-320

Topaz), Bizan-4B, Nickel-KM IFF, (II) MR-320

Topaz-2V, MR-755 Fregat-MA1), Vympel-R2.

Navigation: (I) Don, ARP-50R, (II) MR-212

Vaygach.

Fire control: (I) 4R-33 (SAM), Bar (CIWS), Burya

(Smerch), Drakon (torpedo), MR-123 Vympel

(gun).

Sonar: (I) MG-322T Amgun, (I/II) MG-339T
Shelon, KMG-12 Kassandra, MGS-407K.; (II)
MGK-335 Platina.

Merkuriy

Class: Merukuriy Project 20386 (FFLG)

Country of Origin: Russia

Operators: Russia

Active: 0

Building: 1

Name (Pennant Number): DERZKIY.

SPECIFICATION

Displacement, tons: 3,000 standard, 3,400 full.

Length, feet (meters): 357' 7"(109) oa.

Beam, feet (meters): 49'3" (15) oa.

Draft, feet (meters): 14'1" (4.3).

Speed, knots: 30.

Range, miles: 5,000 at 14 kts.

Complement: 80 (14 Officers, 66 Enlisted).

ARMAMENT

Missiles:

2 x 4 (8) UKSK VLS battery supporting Kalibr missile family, including A/S – 91RT Otvet/Club-N; SSM - 3K55 Oniks/SS-N-26 Strobile, 3M14K Kalibr/SS-N-27 Sizzler, 3K22 Zirkon/SS-N-33. SAM – 2 x 8 (16) 3K96 Redut cells for 16 9M96/SA-21 Growler or 64 9M100 Vityaz/SA-10 Grumble.

Guns: 1 x 3.9-in/100mm A-190 gun, 2 x 30mm AK-301 CIWS.

RECOGNITION FEATURES

- Level maindeck runs from bow to stern, with break by superstructure.
- Stealthy characteristics include angled bridge superstructure.
- 3.9-in gun mounted in A position.
- VLS battery sited on forecastle forward of 3-in gun.
- Tripod mast mounted atop superstructure, aft of bridge.
- Dual round black-tipped funnels atop superstructure, sited aft of midships.
- CIWS turrets mounted tandem, port and starboard, at aft end of superstructure.

Torpedoes: 2 x 4 (8) 12.75-in/324mm SM-588 Paket NK launchers for 8 MTT torpedoes, M-15 anti-torpedoes.

Decoys: TK-25-2 ESM, 4 x KT-216 PK-10 decoy launchers.

SENSORS

Air search: MFRLK-20386 radar complex.

Navigation: MR-231-3, Chardash-20380.

Fire control: 5P-10-02 Puma-02 (gun), MR-123-02 Sfera (CIWS).

Sonars: MGK-335EM-03, Minotavr-ISPN-M.

AIR SUPPORT

Helicopter: 1 x Ka-27 Helix

Nanuchka III

Class: Nanuchka III Project 12341 Ovod (FFL)

US Navy Photo

Country of Origin: Soviet Union

Operators: Russia

Active: 10

Name (Pennant Number): RASSVET, ZYB', GEYZER, PASSAT, LIVIEN, SMERCH, INEY, RAZLIV.

SPECIFICATION

Displacement, tons: 639 standard, 730 full.

Length, feet (meters): 194'7" (59.3) oa.

Beam, feet (meters): 38'9" (11.8) oa.

Draft, feet (meters): 10'1" (3.08).

Speed, knots: 34.

Range, miles: 3,500 at 12 kts, 2,100 at 18 kts.

Complement: 64 (10 Officers, 54 Enlisted).

ARMAMENT

Missiles: SSM - 2 x 4 (8) 3M24 Uran/SS-N-25 Switchblade; SAM -

1 x 2 ZIF-122 34K33 Osa launchers for (20) 9M33/SA-N-4 Gecko.

Guns: 1 x 3-in/76mm AK-176 gun, 1 x 30mm AK-630M CIWS.

RECOGNITION FEATURES

- Continuous maindeck running from bow to stern
- Distinctive tubular SSM launchers angled forward, mounted port and starboard of bridge superstructure.
- Missile launcher mounted in A position.
- 3-in gun mounted in Y position.
- Large radar aerial mounted atop bridge superstructure.
- Lattice mainmast mounted at aft end of bridge superstructure.

Decoys: 4-6 KT-216 launchers for PK-10 decoys.

SENSORS

Air search: Titanit radar complex, 34K1 Monolit, MRP-11-12 Zaliv, Nikhrom-RRM, Nickel-KM IFF

Navigation: Pechora, Mius.

Fire control: 4R-33A (SAM), MR-123 Vympel (gun).

Parchim

Class: Parchim Project 1331M (FFLG)

Country of Origin: East Germany

Operators: Russia

Active: 6

Name (Pennant Number): URENGOY, KAZANETS, KABARDINO-BALKARIYA, KALMYKIYA, ZELENODOLSK, ALEKSIN

SPECIFICATION

Displacement, tons: 856 standard, 935 full.

Length, feet (meters): 246'9" (75.2) oa.

Beam, feet (meters): 32'1" (9.78) oa.

Draft, feet (meters): 8'8" (2.65).

Speed, knots: 24.5.

Range, miles: 2,500 at 12 kts.

Complement: 90 (9 Officers, 81 Enlisted).

ARMAMENT

Missiles: A/S – 2 x 12 (96) RBU-6000 Smerch-2; SAM – 2 x 4 MTU-4U Strela-2M or Strela-3 launchers for (16) 9M32M/SA-7 Grail or 9M36/SA-14 Gremlin.

Guns: 1 x 3-in/76mm AK-176M, 1 x 30mm AK-630M CIWS.

Depth charges: 10.

Torpedoes: 2 x 2 (4) 12-in/533mm tubes.

RECOGNITION FEATURES

- High bow with maindeck break at superstructure.
- Stepped superstructure with lattice mainmast atop central superstructure, aft of bridge.
- CIWS mounted in B position.
- 3-in gun mounted in Y position.
- Depth charge launcher mounted forward of bridge, after of CIWS.
- Quad missile launcher mounted at aft end of superstructure superstructure.
- Lattice mainmast atop central superstructure. Y-shaped in profile lattice mast protruding aft.
- Enclosed secondary mast fitted after superstructure supports radar aerial.

Decoys: Bizan-4B ECM, 2 x KL-101 launchers for PK-16 decoys.

SENSORS

Air/surface search: MR-352 Pozitiv.

Navigation: MR.212/201-3 Vaygach.

Fire control: MR-123 Vympel (gun), Burya (Smerch).

Sonars: MGK-335MS Platina-MS, MG-349 Rosy-K, MG-35 Shtil.

Steregushchiy

Class: Steregushchiy Project 20380 (FFLG)

Alex Fedorov Photo (CC BY-SA 4.0)

Country of Origin: Russia	
Operators: Russia	

Active: 10
Building: 3
Planned: 18

Name (Pennant Number): STEREGUSHCHY (530), SOOBRAZITLENY (531), BOYKY (532), SOVERSHENNY (333), STOYKY (545), GROMKY (335), MERKURIY (535), STROGIY, ADLAR TSYDENZHAPOV (339), REZKIY (343), GROZNIY, BRAVIY.

SPECIFICATION

Displacement, tons: 1800 standard, 2250 full.

Length, feet (meters): 342'10" (104.5) oa.

Beam, feet (meters): 42'8" (13) oa.

Draft, feet (meters): 17'11" (5.45).

Speed, knots: 27.

Range, miles: 4,000 at 14 kts.

Complement: 99 (14 Officers, 85 Enlisted).

ARMAMENT

Missiles: SAM – 3 x 4 (12) 3K96 Redut cells for 32 9M96/SA-21 Growler or 48 9M100 Vityaz/SA-10 Grumble, 1 x 8 3M87 launcher for (64) 9M311 (CIWS); SSM - 2 x 4 (8) 3M24 Uran/SS-N-25 Switchblade.

Guns: 1 x 3.9-in/100mm A-190 gun, 2 x 30mm AK-630M CIWS. 2 x 14.5mm MTPU-1 Zhalo.

Torpedoes: 2 x 4 (8) 12.75-in/324mm SM-588 Paket NK launchers for 8 MTT torpedoes, M-15 anti-torpedoes.

Depth Charges: 2 x 2 (4) 45mm DP-64 launchers.

Decoys: TK-25-2 ESM, 4 x KT-216 PK-10 decoy launchers.

SENSORS

Air search: 5P-20K-A Monument-A, 5P-27M Furke-2, Sandal-V, Parol IFF.

Navigation: MR-231, MR-231-2, PAL-N.

Fire control: 5P-10-02 Puma-02 (gun), MR-123-02 Sfera (CIWS), 3R14N (Kalibr).

Sonars: Zarya-2, Minotavr-ISPN-M, Anapa GISZ, Anapa-M anti-saboteur.

AIR SUPPORT

Helicopter: 1 x Ka-27 Helix

79

Sviyazhsk

Class: Sviyazhsk Project 21630 Buyan/ Project 21631 Buyan-M (FFLG)

Ministry of Defense of Russia Photo

Country of Origin: Russia

Operators: Russia

Active: (21630) 3, (21631) 9 + 1 fitting out

Building: 2

Name (Pennant Number): (21630) ASTRAKHAN, VOLGODONSK, MAHACHKALA; (21631) GRAD SVIYAZHSK (631), UGLICH (632), VELIKIY USTYUG (633), ZELENY DOL (634), SERPUKHOV (635), VYSHNIY VOLOCHYOK (636), OREKHOVO-ZUYEVO (637), INGUSHETIYA (638), GRAYVORON (639), GRAD (640), NARO-FOMINSK (641), STAVROPOL (642)

SPECIFICATION

Displacement, tons: 949

Length, feet (meters): 246 (75) oa.

Beam, feet (meters): 36'1" (11) oa.

Draft, feet (meters): 8'2" (2.5).

Speed, knots: 26.

Range, miles: 2,500 at 12 kts.

Complement: 52.

ARMAMENT

Missiles: 1 x 8 (8) UKSK VLS battery supporting Kalibr missile family, including A/S – 91RT Otvet/Club-N; SSM - 3K55 Oniks/SS-N-26 Strobile, 3M14K Kalibr/SS-N-27 Sizzler, 3K22 Zirkon/SS-N-33. SAM – 2 x 6 3M-47 Gibka Igla-1M, 1 x 8 Pantsir-M CIWS.

Guns: 3.9-in/100mm AK-190 naval gun, 2 x 6 30mm AK-630M CIWS, 2 x 14.5mm MTPU-1 Zhalo MG.

RECOGNITION FEATURES

- Level forecastle with hull chine running from mid-forecastle to stern.
- Superstructure descends in steps to flight deck at stern.
- 3.9-in gun mounted in A position.
- Pozitiv-M radome aerial mounted atop mast after bridge, atop superstructure.
- Laska radar mounted atop forward end of bridge.
- CIWS mounted port and starboard in X position, aft of bridge superstructure.

Note: Distinguished by Pozitiv-M radome atop mast.

Decoys: 2 – 10 PL-10 decoy launchers, TK-25 radar jammers

SENSORS

Air search: 5P-26M Pozitiv-M.

Navigation: MR-231.

Fire control: 5P-10-03 Laska (gun), MP-123-02, 3R14N (Kalibr)

Sonars: MG-757 Anapa-M anti-saboteur sonar.

Tarantul I/II/III

Class: Tarantul I/II/III 12411/12411T/12417 Molniya (FFLG)

Alin2808 Photo (CC BY-SA 4.0)

Country of Origin: Soviet Union

Operators: Russia

Active: 19 (I) 2, (II) 17.

Name (Pennant Number): (I) STUPINETS, R-257, (II) BURYA, R-261, ZARECHNIY, NABEREZHNYE CHELNY, IVANOVETS, R-297, R-298, DIMITROVGRAD, R-11, R-14, MORSHANSK, R-18, R-19, R-20, R-24, CHUVASHIYA, R-29.

SPECIFICATION

Displacement, tons: (I) 436 standard, 493 full, (II) 392 standard, 469 full, (III) 435 standard, 495 full.

Length, feet (meters): (56.1) oa.

Beam, feet (meters): (10.2) oa.

Draft, feet (meters): (2.5).

Speed, knots: 42.

Range, miles:(I)1,600 (II/III) 1,800 at 13 kts, 400 at 36 kts.

Complement: (I) 40 (5 Officers, 35 Enlisted), (II/III) 41 (5 Officers, 36 Enlisted).

ARMAMENT

Missiles: SAM – (I/II) 1 x 4 MTU-4US Strela-3M or 9k310 Igla-1 for (16) 9M313/SA-18 Grouse (II) or 9M36/SA-14 Gremlin. SSM - (I) 2 x 2 KT-152 launchers for (4) 3M80/82 Moskit/SS-N-22 Sunburn, (II/III) 2 x 2 KT-138 launchers for (4) P-15M Termit/SS-N-2 Styx.

Guns: 1 x 3-in/76mm AK-176 gun, (I/II) 2 x 30mm AK-630M CIWS.

RECOGNITION FEATURES

- Maindeck runs continuously from bow to stern.
- 3-in gun mounted in A position.
- Forward-angled SSM tubular launchers mounted on maindeck in pairs, port and starboard amidships along bridge superstructure.
- CIWS mounted in tandem port and starboard at aft end of aft superstructure.
- Aft-angled mainmast mounted atop bridge superstructure, after bridge and radar aerial.

Decoys: Vympel-R2 ESW, 2 x KL-101 launchers for PK-16 decoys.

SENSORS

Air search: 34K1 Monolit radar complex, MR-352 Pozitiv.

Navigation: Don.

Fire control: MR-123 Vympel-A (gun).

Uragan

Class: Uragan Project 22800 Karakurt (FFLG)

Country of Origin: Russia

Operators: Russia

Active: 4 + 1 in sea trials + 8 launched

Building: 4

Name (Pennant Number): MYTISHCHI (567), SOVETSK (577), ODINTSOVO (584), BURYA, TSIKLON, ASKOLD, AMUR, TUCHA, TAIFUN, KOZELSK, OKHOTSK, VIKHR, RZHEV, UDOMLYA, PAVLOVSK, USSURIYSK (204).

SPECIFICATION

Displacement, tons: 800 standard.

Length, feet (meters): 219'10" (67) oa.

Beam, feet (meters): 36'1" (11) oa.

Draft, feet (meters): 10'10" (3.3).

Speed, knots: 30.

Range, miles: 2,500.

Complement: 39.

ARMAMENT

Missiles: 1 x 8 (8) UKSK VLS battery supporting Kalibr missile family, including A/S – 91RT Otvet/Club-N; SSM - 3K55 Oniks/SS-N-26 Strobile, 3M14K Kalibr/SS-N-27 Sizzler, 3K22 Zirkon/SS-N-33; SAM – 1 x 8 Pantsir-M CIWS.

RECOGNITION FEATURES

- Maindeck runs from bow to stern.
- VLS battery fitted into forecastle.
- 3-in gun mounted in A position.
- Pozitiv-M aerial radome mounted atop bridge superstructure, forward of mast.
- Integrated mast atop superstructure supports 4 radar aerials.
- Bridge juts out above inward sloped superstructure.

Guns: 1 x 3-in/76.2mm AK-176MA gun, 2 x 6 30mm AK-630M CIWS, 2 x 12.7mm 6P58 Kord MG.

Decoys: MP-405-1 ESM; 4 x KT-216 launchers for PK-10 decoys.

SENSORS

Air search: KRS-27M Mineral. Pozitiv-MK.

Navigation: Pal-N-4.

Fire control: MR-123-02/3 Bagira (gun), 3R14N (Kalibr), 5P-10-03 Laska (CIWS).

AIR SUPPORT

Unmanned: 1 x Orlan-10 UAV

Mine Warfare Ships

Avenger

US Navy Photo

Class: Avenger (MCM)

Country of Origin: America

Operators: America

Active: 8

Name (Pennant Number): SENTRY (3), DEVASTATOR (6), PATRIOT (7), PIONEER (9), WARRIOR (10), GLADIATOR (11), DEXTROUS (13), CHIEF (14).

SPECIFICATION

Displacement, tons: 1,312.

Length, feet (meters): 224 (68) oa.

Beam, feet (meters): 39 (12) oa.

Draft, feet (meters): 15 (4.6).

Speed, knots: 14.

Complement: 84 (8 Officers, 76 Enlisted)

ARMAMENT

Guns: 2 x.M2HB 50.cal MG, 2 x M60 7.62 MG, 2 x Mk 19 grenade launchers.

Mines: AN/SLQ-48 mine neutralization system, AN/SQL-37(V)3 Magnetic/Acoustic.

Decoys: MDG 1701 Magnetometer Degaussing System.

SENSORS

Surface search: AN/SPS-55.

Navigation: AN/SSN-2 PINS, AN/WSN-7.

Sonars: AN/SQQ-32 mine-hunting sonar.

Wochi

Ministry of Defense of Japan Photo

Class: Wochi Type 81/A (MCM)

Country of Origin: China

Operators: China

Active: 14

Name (Pennant Number): (81)
ZHANGJIAGANG (805), JINGJIANG (810),
LIUYANG (839), LUXI (840), (81A)), --- (831),
XIAOYI (841), TAISHAN (842), CHANGSHU
(843), HESHAN (844), QINGZHOU (845),
YUCHENG (846), RENHUAI (847),
XUANWEI (848), WUDI (849),

SPECIFICATION

Displacement, tons: (81) 996; (81A) 1,200.

Length, feet (meters): 213'3" (65); (81A)

222'5" (67.8) oa.

Beam, feet (meters): 32'10" (10) oa.

Draft, feet (meters): 6'7" (2).

Speed, knots: 16.

Complement: 60.

ARMAMENT

Guns: (81) 1 x 37mm Type 76F twin gun, (81A)

1 x 30mm H/PJ-14 CIWS.

Mine countermeasures: Type 316 mechanical

sweep, Type 317 magnetic sweep, Type 318

acoustic sweep, Type 319 infrasonic sweep.

RECOGNITION FEATURES

- High bow and forecastle, with break in maindeck after bridge superstructure, additional break at quarterdeck
- (81) 37mm gun, (81A) 30mm CIWS mounted in A position after forecastle, forward superstructure.
- Mainmast mounted atop aft end of bridge superstructure.
- Black-tipped, aft-sloped funnel site after midships.
- Minesweeping gear mounted on quarterdeck at stern.

Note: Forecastle is shared with predecessor Fushun-class.

Mines: 6.

SENSORS

Navigation:

Sonars: side-scan minesweeping sonar.

UNMANNED SUPPORT

USV: 2 x Pinguin B3

Wosao

WOSAO I MSC

45 meters

Class: Wosao Type 82 (MCM)

Country of Origin: China	
Operators: China	

Active: 16

Name (Pennant Number): 800, 801, 802, 803, 806, 807, 816, 817, 820, 821, 822, 823, 824, 825, RONGJIANG (826), QIONGHAI (827).

SPECIFICATION
Displacement, tons: 400.

Length, feet (meters): 147 (44.8) oa.

Beam, feet (meters): 20'4" (6.2) oa.

Draft, feet (meters): 7'7" (2.3).

Speed, knots: 15.

Range, miles: 500 at 8 kts.

Complement: 28.

ARMAMENT
Guns: 1 x 37mm Type 61 twin gun.

RECOGNITION FEATURES
- High bow with maindeck running continuously from bow to stern without break.
- Dual funnels mounted after superstructure, forward of quarterdeck, oriented horizontal and aft.
- 37mm gun mounted in A position.
- Mast mounted at aft end of bridge superstructure.
- Minesweeping gear mounted on quarterdeck at stern.

Note: Wosao hulls are constructed of low-magnetic steel..

Mine countermeasures: Type 317 magnetic sweep, Type 318 mechanical sweep, Type 318 acoustic sweep, Type 319 infrasonic sweep.

Mines: 6.

SENSORS
Navigation: Type 753

Wozang

Class: Wozang Type 82II (MCM)

Country of Origin: China

Operators: China

Active: 6

Name (Pennant Number): HUOQIU (804), RUDONG (808), KAIPING (809), RONGCHENG (811), DONGGANG (814), KUNSHAN (818).

SPECIFICATION

Displacement, tons: 575.

Length, feet (meters): 180'5" (55) oa.

Beam, feet (meters): 30'6" (9.3) oa.

Draft, feet (meters): 8'6" (2.6).

Speed, knots: 25.

Complement: 115 (15 Officers, 100 Enlisted).

RECOGNITION FEATURES

- Maindeck runs from bow to break after funnel, additional break before sweep deck.
- Aft-sloped funnel sited after midships, aft of superstructure.
- 25mm gun mounted in A position.
- Pole mainmast centered on superstructure, forward of midships.
- Minesweeping gear mounted on quarterdeck at stern.

ARMAMENT

Guns: 1 x 25mm Type 61 twin gun.

SENSORS

Navigation: Type 732.

Alexandrit

Class: Alexandrit Project 12700 (MCM)

Country of Origin: Soviet Union

Operators: Russia

Active: 7 + 1 in sea trials

Building: 3

Planned: 40

Name (Pennant Number): ALEKSANDR OBUKHOV (507), GEORGIY KURBATOV (631), IVAN ANTONOV (601), VLADIMIR YEMELYANOV (659), YAKOV BALYAEV (616), PYOTR ILYICHEV (543), ANATOLY SHLEMOV, LEV CHERNAVIN, AFANASY IVANNIKOV, POLYARNY, DMITRY LYSOV.

SPECIFICATION

Displacement, tons: 692 standard, 890 full.

Length, feet (meters): 200'2" (61) oa.

Beam, feet (meters): 33'6" (10.2) oa.

Draft, feet (meters): 8'10" (2.7).

Speed, knots: 16.5.

Range, miles: 2,770 at 13 kts, 1,430 at 15.9 kts.

Complement: 51

ARMAMENT

Missiles: SAM – 2 x 4 (8) Igla launchers for (8) 9M39/SA-N-10 Grouse.

Guns: 1 x 30mm AK-306 CIWS, 1 x 14.5mm MTPU-1 Zhalo MG (IVAN ANTONOV,

RECOGNITION FEATURES

- Bow level with maindeck, which runs to break before sweep deck.
- CIWS mounted in A position.
- Aft-angled lattice mast mounted atop aft end of superstructure.
- Pyramidal funnel fitted at aft end of superstructure, before sweeping gear.

Note: Hull is comprised of monolithic fiberglass.

VLADIMIR EMELYANOV) 2 x 12.7mm 6P58 Kord MG.

Mines: UDM, UDM-2, UDM-500, MTPK-1, MTPK-2, MRPK-1 PMR-1, PMR-2.

Mine countermeasures: Diamond system, OUKT-B contact sweep, PKT-B contact sweep, Zhelatin sweep, ShAT-U acoustic sweep.

SENSORS

Navigation: PAL-N.

Sonars: Anapa anti-saboteur, Altyn-M GISZ

UNMANNED CRAFT

USV: 1 x Skanda.

Gorya

Class: Gorya Project 12660 Rubin (MCM)

Country of Origin: Soviet Union

Operators: Russia

Active: 2

Name (Pennant Number): ZHELEZNYAKOV (901), VLADIMIR GUMANENKO (811).

SPECIFICATION

Displacement, tons: 1,070 standard, 1,150 full.

Length, feet (meters): 222'5" (67.8) oa.

Beam, feet (meters): 36'1" (11) oa.

Draft, feet (meters): 10'2" (3.1).

Speed, knots: 15.7.

Range, miles: 1,500 at 12 kts.

Complement: 68 (7 Officers, 61 Enlisted)

ARMAMENT

Missiles: SAM – 2 x 4 (8) 9K34 Strela-3 launchers for 9M36/SA-N-8 Gecko.

Guns: 1 x 3-in/76mm AK-176M gun, 1 x 30mm AK-630M CIWS.

Mines: 16.

Mine countermeasures: 2 x 4 (8) Gyurza anti-mine complex launchers, Ketmen search/removal device, KTK-1 contact sweep, TEM-3M magnetic sweep, AT-3 acoustic sweep, ShZ-3 detonating chord.

Decoys: 2 x KL-101 launchers for PK-16 decoys.

RECOGNITION FEATURES

- Level bow with maindeck break at superstructure, stepped break after superstructure for quarterdeck and sweep deck at stern.
- 3-in gun mounted in A position.
- CIWS mounted in Y position.
- Tripod mainmast mounted atop bridge roof supporting short pole mast at aft end.
- Lifeboats in davits port and starboard, after midships, atop superstructure.
- Minesweeping gear on sweep deck at stern.

SENSORS

Navigation: MR-212/201 Vaygach-U.

Fire control: MR-123-01 Vympel-A (gun).

Sonars: MG-7 Braslet anti-saboteur, MG-99 Kabarga-A3 mine-search.

Lida

Class: Lida Project 10750 Sapfir (MCM)

Ministry of Defense of Russia Photo

Country of Origin: Soviet Union

Operators: Russia

Active: 7

Name (Pennant Number): RT-57 (350), RT-248 (352), VASILY POLYAKOV (354), VICTOR SIGALOV (355), LEONID PEREPECH (356), RT-233 (357), RT-234 (358).

SPECIFICATION
Displacement, tons: 85 light, 131 standard, 135 full.

Length, feet (meters): 103'4" (31.45) oa.

Beam, feet (meters): 21'4" (6.5) oa.

Draft, feet (meters): 5' (1.58).

Speed, knots: 12.5.

Range, miles: 210 at 12.5 kts, 400 at 10 kts.

Complement: 14 (1 Officer, 13 Enlisted)

ARMAMENT
Missiles: SAM – 1 x 8 K310 Igla-1 launchers for 9M313/SA-N-10 Grouse.

Guns: 1 x 6 54 cal/30mm AK-306.

Mines: 4.

RECOGNITION FEATURES
- Swept bow with maindeck running from bow to stern.
- CIWS mounted in A position.
- Bridge superstructure mounted after forecastle.
- Exhaust vane mounted after bridge, forward of midships.
- Navigation radar mounted atop exhaust vane.
- Wire mainmast mounted after of exhaust vane, on aft end of bridge superstructure.
- Lifeboats in davits port and starboard, forward midships, atop superstructure.
- Minesweeping gear on sweep deck at stern.

Mine countermeasures: GKT-3MO contact sweep, SEMT-1 electromagnetic sweep, AT-6 acoustic sweep.

SENSORS
Navigation: MR-231-2 Liman, Bras.

Fire control: Kolonka-219-1 (gun).

Sonars: MG-99A1 Kabarga-A3 mine-search.

Natya

Wikimedia Commons Photo

Class: Natya Project 266M/E Akvamarin-M, 02668 Agat (MCM)

Country of Origin: Soviet Union

Operators: Russia

Active: 4, (266M) 2, (266ME) 1, (02668) 1

Name (Pennant Number): (266M) IVAN GOLUBETS (911), KOVROVETS (913); (2066ME) VALENTIN PIKUL (770), (02668) VITZE-ADMIRAL ZAKHARIN (908).

SPECIFICATION

Displacement, tons: (266M) 745 standard, 800 full; (02668) 791 standard, 852 full.

Length, feet (meters):(266M) 200'1" (61); (02668) 201'1" (61.3) oa.

Beam, feet (meters): 33'6" (10.2) oa.

Draft, feet (meters): 9'10" (3).

Speed, knots: (266M) 16.5 (02668) 17.

Range, miles: (266M) 1,500 at 12 kts; (02668) 3,000 at 12 kts.

Complement: 68 (6 Officers, 62 Enlisted); (02668) 60.

ARMAMENT

Missiles: (266ME) 1 x (20) Igla-1 launchers for 9M313/SA-N-10 Grouse.

Guns: 2 x 30mm twin AK-230M or twin AK-306 or AK-630 CIWS; (266M) 2 x 25mm 2M-3M (twin) turrets; (02668) 1 x 30mm AK-306 CIWS, 2 x 14.5mm MTPU-1 Zhalo MG.

Depth charges: 2 x 5 (10) RBU 1200 Uragan or (68) RGB-12.

Mines: (32) BB-1 or (7) KMD-1000 mines; (266ME) 8 UDE mines.

RECOGNITION FEATURES

- Forward pole mast mounted at bow atop short forecastle.
- Maindeck runs from bow to break after CIWS, at quarterdeck.
- CIWS mounted in A and X positions.
- Superstructure fitted forward of midships.
- Lattice mainmast mounted atop aft end of superstructure.
- Black-tipped aft-sloped funnel mounted after superstructure, forward CIWS in X position.
- Lifeboat in davits, mounted starboard side forward of funnel.
- Sweeping gear fitted at stern on quarterdeck.

Mine countermeasures: AT-3 acoustic sweep, BKT contact sweep, KIU-1 sweep, TEM-4 magnetic sweep, ShZ-2 detonating cord; (266ME) AT-2 acoustic sweep, GKT contact sweep, TEM-3 magnetic sweep; (02668) Livadiya sweep.

SENSORS

Air/surface search: MR-302 Rubka/Strut Curve, Don-D/Low Trough.

Navigation: MR-212 Vaygach/Palm Frond.

Fire control: MR-104 Rys/Drum Tilt (CIWS), (266ME) Kolonka (CIWS).

Sonars: MG-69 Lan mine search, MG 79 Mezen hull-mounted mine search, (02668) Livadiya mine search; Anapa-P anti-saboteur.

Sonya

Class: Sonya Project 1265/E Yakhont (MCM)

Country of Origin: Soviet Union

Operators: Russia

Active: 22 (1265) 21 (1265E) 1

Name (Pennant Number): ASTRAKHANETS (107), BT-726 (442), BT-21 (433), MINERALNIE VODY (458), NOVOCHEBOKSARSK (501), LEONID SOBOLEV (510), PAVEL KHENOV (515), BT-232 (525), BT-114 (542), BT-245 (553), BT-256 (560), GERMAN UGRYUMOV (562), BT-100 (565), BT-55 (580), BT-325(586), BT-215 (593), POLYARNY (603), ELNYA (607), KOTELNICH (610), YADRIN (621), KOLOMNA (641), SOLOVETSKIY YUNGA (654).

SPECIFICATION

Displacement, tons: (1265) 427 standard, 460 full; (1265E) 401 standard, 427 full.

Length, feet (meters): (1265) 160'9" (49) (1265E) 161'1" (49.1) oa.

Beam, feet (meters): 28'10" (8.8) oa.

Draft, feet (meters): (1265) 8'2" (2.5), (1265E) 7'10" (2.4).

Speed, knots: 14.

Range, miles: 1,500 at 10 kts.

Complement: 45 (5 Officers, 40 Enlisted)

ARMAMENT

Missiles: SAM - (4) MTU-4 9K34 Strela-3 for 9M36/SA-N-8 Gremlin.

RECOGNITION FEATURES

- Maindeck runs from bow to break at quarterdeck.
- Tripod mast after bridge superstructure supports radar aerials at aft end of superstructure.
- Black-tipped funnel fitted after superstructure, forward quarterdeck.
- Guns mounted in A and X positions; (1265E) CIWS mounted in A and X positions
- Minesweeping gear mounted on quarterdeck at stern.

Note: Sonya-class hulls are wooden to mitigate accidental mine detonation.

Guns: 1 x 25mm (twin) 2M-3M gun, 1 x 30mm AK-230M, 2 x 30mm AK-306 CIWS.

Mines: 6.

Mine countermeasures: GKT-2 contact sweep, PEMT-4 magnetic sweep, ST-2 mangetic sweep, TS-1 sweep; (1265) AT-6 acoustic sweep, KIU-1 Luch mine search, detonation cord; (1265E) AT-2 acoustic sweep, IT-3 sweep.

SENSORS

Navigation: Mius, Don-2 or MR-21/201 Vaygach-U.

Sonars: MG-69 Lan mine search, MG-79 Mezen mine search, MG-7 Braslet anti-saboteur, (1265E) MG-89 mine search.

Patrol Ships

Hainan

Class: Hainan Type 037 (AS)

Country of Origin: China

Operators: China

Active: 67

Name (Pennant Number): 601, 602, 603, 604, 605, 606, 607, 608, 609, 610, 622, 625, 626, 627, 628, 629, 639, 650, 673, 674, 677, 681, 682, 683, 684, 685, 686, 687, 689, 690, 691, 692, 694, 695, 696, 698, 699, 700, 701, 702, 703, 704, 705, 706, 707, 708, 709, 721, 722, 723, 724, 725, 726, 727, 728, 729, 730, 731, 732, 733, 734, 735, 736, 737, 738, 739, 740, 741, 742.

SPECIFICATION
Displacement, tons: 430.

Length, feet (meters): 192'10" (58.8) oa.

Beam, feet (meters): 21'4" (7.2) oa.

Draft, feet (meters): 7'3" (2.2).

Speed, knots: 30.5.

Complement: 70.

ARMAMENT
Guns: 2 x 57mm Type 66 twin guns, 2 x25mm Type 61 twin MG.

RECOGNITION FEATURES

- High bow with long forecastle, maindeck runs continuously from bow to stern.
- Depth charge launchers mounted in tandem on forecastle.
- 57mm guns mounted in A and Y positions.
- 25mm guns mounted in B and X positions.
- Lattice mainmast fitted at aft end of bridge superstructure, forward gap between superstructures at midships.

Note: Houxin class is missile-armed variant of Hainan class.

Mines: 18 KB mines.

Mortars: 4 x 5 (20) RBU-1200 launchers for 20 BGB depth charges and 20 MGB depth charges.

SENSORS
Surface search: Type 351/Pot Head

Navigation: Type 723.

Sonars: MG-11/Stag Hoof hull mounted, or SJD-3 active

94

Haiqing

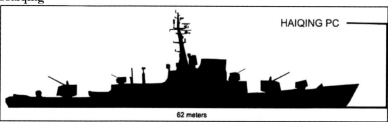

HAIQING PC

62 meters

Class: Haiqing Type 37I/IS (PSC)

US Navy Image

Country of Origin: China	
Operators: China	

Active: 27 (37I) 4, (47IS) 23

Name (Pennant Number): (37I) 688, 693, 694, 697; (37IS) 611, 612, 613, 614, 619, 631, 632, 633, 634, 635, 710, 711, 712, 743, 744, 761, 762, 763, 786, 787, 788, 789.

SPECIFICATION

Displacement, tons: (37I) 450, (37IS) 478.

Length, feet (meters): 206 (62.8) oa.

Beam, feet (meters): 23'7" (7.2) oa.

Draft, feet (meters): 7'10" (2.4).

Speed, knots: 28, (37IS) 31.5.

Range, miles: 1,750 at 18 kts.

Complement: 71

ARMAMENT

Missiles: (688) SSM – 1 x 4 for (4) YJ-83/CSS-N-8 Saccade.

Guns: 2 x 37mm Type 61/Type 76 twin guns, 2 x 14.5mm Type 69 twin MG.

Mortars: (37IS) 2 x 5 (10) Type 1200 launchers, (37IS) 2 x 6 (12) Type 64 launchers.

Mines: 2 launching rails.

SENSORS

Surface search: Type 352/Square Tie.

Navigation: Type 723.

Fire control: Type 347/Rice Lamp.

Sonar: SS-12 VDS.

RECOGNITION FEATURES

- High bow with long forecastle, maindeck run continuous from bow to stern.
- Depth charge launchers mounted tandem port and starboard on forecastle.
- 37mm twin gun turrets mounted in A and X positions.
- 14.5mm MG mounted in B and Y positions.
- Superstructure sited midships.
- Mast sited after bridge atop superstructure, supporting aerials.

Houbei

Class: Houbei Type 22 (FAC)

US Navy Photo

Country of Origin: China	
Operators: China	

Active: 82

Name (Pennant Number): 2208-2290

SPECIFICATION

Displacement, tons: 220 full.

Length, feet (meters): 139'9" (42.6) oa.

Beam, feet (meters): 40' (12.2) oa.

Draft, feet (meters): 4'11" (1.5).

Speed, knots: 36.

Complement: 12.

ARMAMENT

Missiles: SSM – 2 x 4 (8) YJ-83/CSS-N-8 Saccade.

Guns: 1 x 30mm AK-630 CIWS.

Decoys: 2 x 4 (8) decoy launchers.

SENSORS

Surface search/navigation: H/LJQ-362/Type 362.

Fire control: H/ZFJ-1A (SSM), H/ZGJ-1B (CIWS).

Houjian

Class: Houjian Type37II (PGG)

Tksteven Photo (CC BY 3.0)

Country of Origin: China

Operators: China

Active: 5

Name (Pennant Number): YANGJIANG (770), SHUNDE (771), PANYU (773), LIANJIANG (774), XINHUI (775).

SPECIFICATION
Displacement, tons: 542.

Length, feet (meters): 214'7" (65.4) oa.

Beam, feet (meters): 28'6" (8.7) oa.

Draft, feet (meters): 7'2" (2.4).

Speed, knots: 34.

Ranges, miles: 1,800 at 18 kts.

Complement: 47.

ARMAMENT
Missiles: SSM – 2 x 3 (6) YJ-8A/CSS-N-4 Sardine.

Guns: 1 x 37mm Type 76A twin gun, 1 x Type 038H1 76mm gun, 2 x 30mm Type 69A twin gun.

SENSORS
Surface search: Type 352/Square Tie.

Navigation: Type 723.

Fire control: Type 347/Rice Lamp.

RECOGNITION FEATURES
- Maindeck runs continuously from high bow to stern.
- 37mm gun mounted in A position.
- 30mm guns mounted in Y and X positions.
- Enclosed mast mounted atop bridge superstructure, lattice superstructure mounted at aft end of bridge superstructure.
- Box SSM launchers fitted port and starboard between superstructures, trained forward and outboard.

Houxin

Class: Houxin Type 037IG (PGG)

Country of Origin: China	
Operators: China	

Active: 20

Name (Pennant Number): 651, 652, 653, 654, 655, 656, 751, 752, 753, 754, 755, 756, 757, 758, 759, 760, 764, 765, 766, 767, 768, 769.

SPECIFICATION

Displacement, tons: 478.

Length, feet (meters): 206 (62.8) oa.

Beam, feet (meters): 24 (7.2) oa.

Draft, feet (meters): 7'10" (2.4).

Speed, knots: 28.

Range, miles: 750 at 18 kts.

Complement: 60.

ARMAMENT

Missiles: SSM – (4) YJ-8A/CSS-N-4 Sardine.

Guns: 2 x 37mm Type 76A twin guns, 2 x 14.5mm Type 69 twin MG.

SENSORS

Surface search: Type 352/Square Tie..

Navigation: Type 723.

Fire control: Type 347/Rice Lamp.

RECOGNITION FEATURES

- High bow with long forecastle, maindeck runs continuously from bow to stern.
- 37mm gun mounted in A position.
- 14.5mm MGs mounted in tandem in B position.
- 37mm gun mounted in X position atop aft superstructure.
- 2 forward and outboard-trained twin SSM launchers mounted in tandem on quarterdeck.
- Lattice mainmast fitted at aft end of bridge superstructure, forward gap between superstructures at midships.

Note: Missile-armed version of Hainan class.

Bykov

Class: Bykov Project 22160 (PC)

Country of Origin: Russia

Ministry of Defense of Russia Photo

Operators: Russia

Active: 4

Building: 2

Name (Pennant Number): VASILY BYKOV (368), DMITRIY ROGACHEV (375), PAVEL DERZHAVIN (363), SERGEY KOTOV, VIKTOR VELIKIY, NIKOLAY SIPYAGIN.

SPECIFICATION

Displacement, tons: 1,965 full.

Length, feet (meters): 299'6" (91.3) oa.

Beam, feet (meters): 14'9" (4.5) oa.

Draft, feet (meters): 15'9" (4.8).

Speed, knots: 30.

Range, miles: 6,0000at 16kts.

Complement: 40.

ARMAMENT

Missiles: SSM – 2 x 4 (8) VLS cells for 3M14K Kalibr/SS-N-27 Sizzler. SAM – 1 x 8 9K338 Igla-S (8) 9M432/SA-N-10 Grouse.

Guns: 1 x 3-in/76mm AK-176MA-01 gun, 2 x 14.5mm MTPU-1 Zhalo MG.

Depth Charges: 1 x 55mm D-65 launcher for RG-55M, GRS-55; 2 x 2 (4) 45mm DP-64 launchers for SG_45, FG-45.

Decoys: TK-25E ECM, 1 x KL-121 for PK-10 decoys.

RECOGNITION FEATURES

- Hull chine runs from bow to stern, maindeck level, broken by aft-angled superstructure sited midships.
- 3-in naval gun mounted in A position.
- VLS cells fitted in aft end of superstructure.
- Pozitiv-M radar aerial mounted atop enclosed mast atop sloped bridge superstructure.

SENSORS

Air/surface search: Pozitiv-ME1.

Navigation: Pal-N.

Fire Control: Bagira (gun), 3RP14 (Kalibr)

Sonars: Pallada anti-saboteur, Vinyetka-EM active/passive, MGK-335EM-03 hull-mounted.

AIR SUPPORT

Helicopter: 1 x Ka-27 Helix.

Grachonok

Alex Omen Photo

Class: Grachonok Project 21980 (PC)

Country of Origin: Russia	
Operators: Russia	

Active: 20

Building: 1

Name (Pennant Number): NAKHIMOVETS (P-104), KADET (P-191), YUNARMEETS ZAPOLYARYA (P-340), SUVOROVETS (P-349), KURSANT KIROVETS (P-350), YUNARMEETS KRYMA (P-355), (P-377), YUNARMEETS KAMCHATKI (P-417), YUNARMEETS PRIMORYA (P-420), YUNARMEETS BELOMORYA (P-421), KINEL (P-424), (P-429), VALERIY FEDYANIN (P-430), YUNARMEETS CHUKOTKI (P-431), PAVEL SILAEV (P-433), (P-445), YUNARMEETS TATARSTANA (---), YUNARMEETS DAGESTANA (P-449), YUNARMEETS SAKHALINA (P-450), (P-468), VLADIMIR NOSOV (P-471).

SPECIFICATION

Displacement, tons: 138 full.

Length, feet (meters): 103'0" (31.4) oa.

Beam, feet (meters): 24'3" (7.4) oa.

Draft, feet (meters): 6'1" (1.85).

Speed, knots: 23.

Complement: 8.

ARMAMENT

Missiles: SAM – 1 x 4 Fasta-4M 9M39/ SA-N-8 Gremlin.

Guns: 1 x 14.5mm MTPU-1 Zhalo MG.

Depth Charges: 1 x 45mm DP-64 launcher for SG-45, FG-45, 1 x DP-65 launcher.

RECOGNITION FEATURES

- Hull chine runs angled aft from bow to midships.
- Maindeck runs smoothly from bow to stern
- Bridge superstructure mounted amidships,
- 14.5mm MG mounted in A position.
- VLS cells fitted in forward end of bridge superstructure, forward bridge.
- Wire mainmast mounted atop aft end of bridge.
- Bridge superstructure steps down from bridge after midships.

SENSORS

Air/surface search: MR-231.

Navigation: MR-231 PAL.

Sonar: Kalmar complex, MG-757 Anapa-M antisaboteur.

Gyurza-M

Class: Gyurza-M Project 58155 (PB)

Country of Origin: Ukraine

Operators: Russia

Active: 4

Name (Pennant Number): AKKERMAN (BK 01), KREMENCHUK (BK-04), LUBNY (BK 05), VYSHGOROD (BK 06).

SPECIFICATION
Displacement, tons: 54 full.

Length, feet (meters): 75'6" (23) oa.

Beam, feet (meters): 15'9" (4.8) oa.

Draft, feet (meters): 3'3" (1.0).

Speed, knots: 25.

Range, miles: 900 at 12kts.

Complement: 5.

ARMAMENT
Missiles: 2 x Barrier antitank.

Guns: 2 x 2 (4) 30mm ZTM-1 BM-5M.01

Katran-M CIWS, 2x 30mm KBA-117 grenade

launcher, 1 x 7.62mm PKT MG.

SENSORS
Navigation: Delta-M.

.

RECOGNITION FEATURES
- Hull chine runs from bow to stern, angled from forecastle to maindeck and then level with main deck to stern.
- 30mm guns mounted in A and y positions.
- Slanted bridge mounted amidships, with slanted stucture fitted forward of bridge.
- Radar aerials mounted atop aft-angled mast, mounted atop aft-end o bridge superstructure.

Note: Russia captured four Gyurza-M ships at Berdyansk in February 2022.

Svetlyak

Marko Pislar Photo

Class: Svetlyak Project 1041 (PC)

Country of Origin: Soviet Union

Operators: Russia

Active: 26

Name (Pennant Number): KORSAKOV (PSKR-900), KHOLMSK (PSKR-903), (PSKR-916), YUZHNO-SAKHALINSK (PSKR-918), (PSKR-922), KONDOR (PSK-923), VORON (PSKR-926), UST-LABINSK, BALAKLAVA, VASILI GRYAZEV (PSKR-928), BERKUT (PSKR-929), NEVELSK (PSKR-259), NAKHODKA (PSKR-261), ANATOLII KOROLEV (PSKR-912), ALMAZ (PSKR-913), DERBENT (PSKR-919), SYKTYVKAR (PSKR-920), KYZLYAR (PSKR-921), VALENIN PIKUL (PSKR-924), YAMALETS (PSKR-925), (PSKR-927), KRASNODARETS (PSKR-436), KRYM (PSKR-932), KERCH (PSKR-933), SOCHI.

SPECIFICATION

Displacement, tons: 365, standard, 382 full.

Length, feet (meters): 147'8" (45) wl.

Beam, feet (meters): 30'2" (9.2) oa.

Draft, feet (meters): 8'2" (2.5).

Speed, knots: 32.

Range, miles: 1,500 at 32 kts, 2,200 at 13 kts.

Complement: 28. (4 Officers, 4 Warrant Officers, 20 Enlisted). Accommodation for 44.

ARMAMENT

Missiles: SAM – 16 x 9K338 Igla-S (8) 9M432/SA-N-8 Gremlin.

Guns: 1 x 3-in/76mm AK-176 DP gun, 1 x 30mm AK-630M CIWS.

Torpedoes: 2 x 402mm OTA-40 tubes

RECOGNITION FEATURES

- Semiplaning, round-bilge hull with low spray chine running from bow to midships.
- Maindeck runs from bow to stern.
- 3-in naval gun mounted in B position.
- Bridge mounted after forecastle, forward of midships.
- Bridge superstructure steps up after bridge.
- Wire mainmast mounted atop superstructure, aft of Brudge.
- VLS cells fitted after bridge superstructure.
- Uzh dipping sonar located at stern.

Depth Charges: 2 x 6 (12) 45mm DP-64 launchers.

Electronic: Slyabing, MFD/F.

Decoys: 2 x 16 (32) PK-10 decoys.

SENSORS

Air/surface search: Reyd / Peel Cone.

Fire Control: MR-123 Vympel-AM / Bass Tilt.

Sonars: Uzh HF dipping sonar.

Submarines

Columbia

Class: Columbia (SSBN)

Country of Origin: America	
Operators: America	
Active: 0	
Building: 1	
Planned: 12	

Name (Pennant Number): COLUMBIA (826), WISCONSIN (827), ----

SPECIFICATION
Displacement, tons: 20,810.

Length, feet (meters): 560' (170.7) oa.

Beam, feet (meters): 43' (13.1) oa.

Speed, knots: 10 surfaced; 20 submerged.

Range, miles: unlimited.

Complement: 155.

RECOGNITION FEATURES
- Low hull profile with slight arch to water level from bow to stern.
- Slender fin sited forward of midships, with diving planes fitted at mid-height.
- Dual mast atop fin.
- No vertical tail.

ARMAMENT
Missiles: SLBM - 16 x Trident II/D5 LE with W76 or W88 nuclear warheads.

Torpedoes: 2 x 21-in/533mm tubes for Mk 48.

SENSORS
Surface search/navigation/fire control: SWFTS integrated sensor system.

Sonars: LAB hull-mounted.

Los Angeles

US Navy Photo

Class: Los Angeles (SSN)

Country of Origin: America

Operators: America

Active: 24

Reserve: 1 (722), 2 as moored training ships (701, 711)

Name (Pennant Number): LA JOLLA (701), SAN FRANCISCO (711), KEY WEST (722), HELENA (725), NEWPORT NEWS (750), SAN JUAN (751), PASADENA (752), ALBANY (753), TOPEKA (754), SCRANTON (756), ALEXANDRIA (757), ASHEVILLE (758), JEFFERSON CITY (759), ANNAPOLIS (760), SPRINGFIELD (761), COLUMBUS (762), SANTA FE (763), BOISE (764), MONTPELIER (765), CHARLOTTE (766), HAMPTON (767), HARTFORD (768), TOLEDO (769), TUCSON (770), COLUMBIA (771), GREENEVILLE (772), CHEYENNE (773)

SPECIFICATION

Displacement, tons: 6,082 surfaced, 6,972 submerged.

Length, feet (meters): 362 (110.3) oa.

Beam, feet (meters): 33 (10.1) oa.

Draft, feet (meters): 31 (9.4).

Speed, knots: 20 surfaced; 32 submerged.

Complement: 129

ARMAMENT

Missiles: SLCM – TLAM-N; SSM – TASM. Harpoon.

RECOGNITION FEATURES

- Blunt bow, low profile hull tapers to water level from bow to stern.
- Fin sited forward of midships, with swept diving vanes fitted mid-height and forward.
- Aft vertical rudder with sloping forward edge.

Note: 762, 766, 768, and 772 fitted for Advanced Swimmer Delivery System dry submersibles.

Torpedoes: 4 x 21-in/533mm tubes midships; 37 x Mk 48 torpedo.

Mines: Mk 67 Mobile, Mk 60 Captor minelaying capable.

Decoys: Mk 2 torpedo decoy, WLT-10 countermeasures set.

SENSORS

Surface search/navigation/fire control: BPS 15H/16.

Sonars: (active) BQS-15; (active/passive search & attack) – BQQ-5D/E; (flank array) – BQG-5D (710, 751+); (mine & ice avoidance system) MIDAS (751+); (passive) TB 23/29 thin line array or TB 16 and TB 93 towed array

Ohio

Class: Ohio (SSBN)/(SSGN)

Country of Origin: America

Operators: America

Active: 18

Name (Pennant Number): (SSGN) OHIO 9726),
MICHIGAN (727), FLORIDA (728), GEORGIA
(729); (SSBN) HENRY M JACKSON (730),
ALABAMA (731), ALASKA (732), NEVADA (733),
TENNESSEE (734), PENNSYLVANIA (735),
WEST VIRGINIA (736), KENTUCKY 737),
MARYLAND (738), NEBRASKA (739), RHODE
ISLAND (740), MAINE (741), WYOMING (742),
LOUISIANA (743).

SPECIFICATION

Displacement, tons: 16,600 surfaced, 18,750

submerged.

Length, feet (meters): 560' (170.7) oa.

Beam, feet (meters): 42' (12.8) oa.

Draft, feet (meters): 36'5" (11.1)

Speed, knots: 12 surfaced; 24 submerged.

Range, miles: unlimited.

Complement: 155 (15 Officers, 140 Enlisted).

ARMAMENT

Missiles: (SSBN) (730-733) 24 x Trident I/C4

SLBM; (734+) 24 x Trident II/D5 MIRVed

nuclear warheads; (SSGN) 154 x

missiles/torpedoes TLAMs or Mk 48 torpedoes.

Torpedoes: 4 x 21-in/533mm Mk 68 bow

tubes, Mk 48 torpedoes.

Decoys: 8 launchers for Mk 2 torpedo decoy.

SENSORS

Surface search/navigation/fire control: BPS-

15A/H

US Navy Photo

RECOGNITION FEATURES

- Long, steeply forward-sloped hull
  with gradually-tapering slope aft to
  rudder.
- Tall, thin sail sited forward of
  midships with vertical sides.
- Diving planes mounted forward on
  sail at mid-height.

Note: The Advanced SEAL Delivery
System and dry deck shelter can be
mounted on lockout chamber of Ohio-class
submarines for special operations.

Sonars: (active navigation) – BQR-19;
(active/passive search) – BQS-15; (passive
search) – BQQ-6, BQS-13 spherical array; TB 16
or BQR-23 towed array.

Seawolf

US Department of Defense Photo

Class: Seawolf (SSN)

Country of Origin: America	
Operators: America	

Active: 3

Name (Pennant Number): SEAWOLF (21), CONNECTICUT (22), JIMMY CARTER (23).

SPECIFICATION

Displacement, tons: 8,080 surfaced, 9,142 submerged.

Length, feet (meters): 353' (107.6) (21/22) 452'10" (138) (23) oa.

Beam, feet (meters): 42'4" (12.9) oa.

Draft, feet (meters): 35'10" (10.9)

Speed, knots: 18+ surfaced; 39 submerged.

Complement: 140 (14 Officers, 126 Enlisted)

ARMAMENT

Missiles: up to 50 UGM-109 Tomahawk, UGM-84 Harpoon, Mk 48 torpedoes.

Torpedoes: 8 x 26-in/660mm Mk 48 torpedo.

Mines: 100 instead of torpedoes.

SENSORS

Navigation: BPS-16.

Sonars: AN/BSY-2 Combat system integrates the following (active) – AN/BQS-24; (active/passive) – AN/BBQ-5D bowed spherical with flank array; TB-16 and TB-29 towed arrays.

RECOGNITION FEATURES

- Blunt bow with low profile hull and short aft-angled slope to rudder at stern.
- Sail mounted forward of midships with flat top, rounded, curved forward slope, and vertical aft end.
- Sail omits diving vanes.

Virginia

Class: Virginia (SSN)

Country of Origin: America

Operators: America

Active: 22 (774-795)

Building: 12

Planned: 66

Name (Pennant Number): VIRGINIA (774),
TEXAS (775), HAWAII (776), NORTH
CAROLINA (777), NEW HAMPSHIRE (778),
NEW MEXICO (779), MISSOURI (780),
CALIFORNIA (781), MISSISSIPPI (782),
MINNESOTA (783), NORTH DAKOTA (784),
JOHN WARNER (785), ILLINOIS (786),
WASHINGTON (787), COLORADO (788),
INDIANA (789), SOUTH DAKOTA (790),
DELAWARE (791), VERMONT (792),
OREGON (793), MONTANA (794), HYMAN
RICKOVER (795), NEW JERSEY (796), IOWA
(797), MASSACHUSETTS (798), IDAHO (799),
ARKANSAS (800), UTAH (801), OKLAHOMA
(802), ARIZONA (803), BARB (804), TANG
(805), WAHOO (806), SILVERSIDES (807),
JOHN H. DALTON (808), LONG ISLAND
(809), SAN FRANCISCO (810), ---(811).

SPECIFICATION

Displacement, tons: 7,800 submerged.

Length, feet (meters): 377' (114.8) oa.

Beam, feet (meters): 34' (10.4) oa.

Speed, knots: 25 submerged.

Range, miles: unlimited.

Complement: 135 (15 Officers, 120 Enlisted).

US Navy Photo

RECOGNITION FEATURES

- Blunt bow, low profile pressure hull.
- Low hull profile tapered with slight
  arch midships, down to water level
  from bow to stern.
- Slender fin, with vertical leading and
  aft edges, sited forward of midships.
- Three masts atop fin, photonic mast
  replacing traditional periscope sited
  between two identical cylinders.
- Tall rudder aft with sloping forward
  edge.

ARMAMENT

Missiles: (12) Mk 45 VLS containing UGM-109
Tomahawk, UGM-84 Harpoon. ((784+) (12) Mk
45 VLS.

Torpedoes: 4 x 21-in/533 mm tubes with Mk
48 torpedoes or mines.

Decoys: Mk 3/Mk 4 acoustic device
countermeasure.

SENSORS

Navigation: LCCA sonar.

Sonars: (active/passive) BQQ-10 hull-mounted;
TB-16 or TB-34 VDS, TB-29 or TB-33 VDS,
(784+) LAB sonar array.

Han

US Navy Photo

Class: Han Type 091 (SSN)

Country of Origin: China	
Operators: China	

Active: 3

Name (Pennant Number): 403, 404, 405.

SPECIFICATION

Displacement, tons: 4,500 surfaced, 5,550 submerged.

Length, feet (meters): 321'6" (98) (401-402), 347'10" (106) (403-405) oa.

Beam, feet (meters): 32'10" (10) oa.

Draft, feet (meters): 24'3" (7.4).

Speed, knots: 12 surfaced; 25 submerged.

Complement: 75.

ARMAMENT

Missiles: VLS comprised of ASCM – YJ-8/C-801 Eagle Strike.

Torpedoes: 6 x 21-in/533mm bow tubes; 18 x Yu-3/SET-65E and Yu-1/Type 63-51 torpedoes.

Mines: capacity for 36 mines.

SENSORS

Surface search: MRP-25 Snoop Tray.

Sonars: (active/passive search and attack) MG-10M Feniks/Trout Cheek hull-mounted; (active) SQZ-3 hull-mounted, (passive) Type H/SQ2-262B hull-mounted, H/SQC-1 hull-mounted.

RECOGNITION FEATURES

- Teardrop-shaped hull with relatively high profile.
- Fin sited forward of midships with diving planes at forward edge, above mid-height.
- Fin has vertical forward edge, top sloping down towards aft end and sloping after edge, curved at the bottom.
- Tall rudder with sloping forward edge and vertical aft edge.
- SSM tubes fitted aft of the fin.

Jin

Class: Jin Type 094/A (SSBN)

Country of Origin: China

Operators: China

Active: 6 (94) 4 (94A) 2

Name (Pennant Number): (94) --- (411), CHANGZHENG 10 (412), CHANGZHENG 11 (413), CHANGZHENG 18 (421), (94A) ---, ---.

SPECIFICATION
Displacement, tons: 8,000 surfaced, 11,000 submerged.

Length, feet (meters): 442'11" (137) oa.

Beam, feet (meters): 41' (10) oa.

Draft, feet (meters): 38'9" (11.8).

Speed, knots: 25 submerged.

Range, miles: unlimited.

Complement: 130.

ARMAMENT
Missiles: (94) (12) VLS comprised of SLBM – JL-2/CSS-NX-14 with 1 MT or 3-8 MIRV with 20/90/150 kT nuclear warheads; (94A) (16) VLS comprised of SLBM – JL-2A/CSS-NX-14 with

RECOGNITION FEATURES
- Blunt, rounded, low bow.
- Slender, profile fin sited forward of midships.
- Large driving planes on fin at leading edge, mid-height.
- Raised flat-topped missile casing aft of the fin with forward end molded round aft edge of fin. Missile casing runs straight for less than half the distance to the stern where it tapers away.
- Rudder, with flat, protruding aft edge, visible aft.

Note: (094A) distinguished by modified, rounder sail and omission of navigation windows.

1 MT or 3-8 MIRV with 20/90/150 kT nuclear warheads.

SENSORS
Surface search: MRK-50/Snoop Tray.

Sonars: (active/passive) sonar bow-mounted, (passive) SQG-04 hull-mounted, Type H/SQ2-262B hull-mounted.

Ming

Mike1979 Russia Photo (CC BY-SA 4.0)

Class: Ming Type 035B/G (SSK)

Country of Origin: China	
Operators: China	

Active: 13 (35B) 5 (35G) 8

Name (Pennant Number): (35B) 309, 310, 311, 312, 313, (35G) 359, 360, 362, 363, 305, 306, 307, 308

SPECIFICATION

Displacement, tons: 2,110 submerged.

Length, feet (meters): 249'4" (76), 255'11" (78) (308 only) oa.

Beam, feet (meters): 24'11" (7.6) oa.

Draught, feet (meters): 34'1" (10.4).

Speed, knots: 15 surfaced, 18.5 submerged.

Complement: 55 (9 Officers, 46 Enlisted).

ARMAMENT

Missiles: (35B) YJ-82/C-801Q Sardine.

Torpedoes: (35A) 6 x 21-in/533 mm tubes, (35B) 8 x 21-in/533mm tubes) for 14 Yu-3 torpedoes or 28 mines.

Decoys: Type 921A/Golf Ball ESM; noisemaker/bubble screen decoy.

SENSORS

Surface search: (35A) Snoop Plate, (35B) MRK-50E Kaskad/Snoop Tray.

Sonars: (active) (35G) H/SQ2-262C/Pike Jaw, (35B) SQB-2 generic acoustic intercept; (active/passive) SQC-1/DSUV 2H/22 hull-mounted; (passive) SQB-2/DUUX 5 Fenelon hull-mounted, Flank Array towed array

Qing

HI Sutton Photo

Class: Qing Type 032 (SSK)

Country of Origin: China	
Operators: China	

Active: 1

Name (Pennant Number): 201

SPECIFICATION

Displacement, tons: 3,797 surfaced, 6,628 submerged.

Length, feet (meters): 301'10" (92) oa.

Beam, feet (meters): 32'10" (10) oa.

Draft, feet (meters): 22'8" (6.9).

Speed, knots: 10 surface, 14 submerged.

Complement: 85.

ARMAMENT

Missiles: 7 VLS cells able to launch SLBM – JL-2A with 1 Mt nuclear warheads or 3-4 90 kt MIRV warheads, SSM – JL-18B, CJ-20A.

Torpedoes: 1 x 21-in/533 mm for Yu-6 or Yu-8 torpedoes, 1 x 25.6-in/650mm tubes.

Decoys: Type 921A ESM.

SENSORS

Surface search: MRK-50/Snoop Tray.

Sonars: (active/passive) sonar bow-mounted, (passive) SQG-04 hull-mounted.

RECOGNITION FEATURES

- Blunt bow, teardrop-shaped hull.
- High-profile in water, with large, elongated fin sited midships.
- 3 VLS cells located in fin, equipped with SLBMs, 4 VLS cells located in hull, equipped with SSMs.
- Tall, vertical tail.
- Torpedo tubes sited on bow, 21-in/533mm tube on port side, and 25.6

Note: Equipped with AIP engine system and integral submarine escape pod.

Note: Qing-class' unusual weapons and technology configuration and single vessel in class underscored by testing and evaluation mission.

Shang

Class: Shang Type 093 (SSN)

Country of Origin: China

Operators: China

Active: 8

Name (Pennant Number): (093)
CHANGZHENG 7 (407), CHANGZHENG 8
(408), (093A) CHANGZHENG 13 (413),
CHANGZHENG 14 (414), (093B)
CHANGZHENG 15 (415), CHANGZHENG 16
(416), CHANGZHENG 17 (417),
CHANGZHENG 18 (418).

RECOGNITION FEATURES

- Teardrop-shaped hull with relatively high profile.
- Fin sited forward of midships with diving planes at forward edge, above mid-height, below navigation windows.
- Fin has vertical forward edge, top sloping down towards aft end.
- Tall rudder with sloping forward edge and sloping aft edge.

Note: Similar in appearance to Russia's Victor III submarine.

SPECIFICATION

Displacement, tons: 7,000 submerged.

Length, feet (meters): 351' (107) oa.

Beam, feet (meters): 36'1" (11) oa.

Draft, feet (meters): 24'7" (7.5).

Speed, knots: 30 submerged.

Complement: 100.

ARMAMENT

Missiles: (22) projectiles comprised of ASCM –
YJ-18/CH-SS-NX-13, YJ-82/C-801Q Sardine,
Yu-6 torpedoes.
Torpedoes: 6 x 21-in/533 mm tubes for Yu-6

torpedoes.

Decoys: Type 921A ESM

SENSORS

Surface search: MRP-25 Snoop Tray.

Sonars: (active/passive search and attack) MG-

10M Feniks/Trout Cheek hull-mounted; (active)

SQZ-3 hull-mounted, (passive) Type H/SQ2-

262B hull-mounted, H/SQC-1 hull-mounted.

Song

Class: Song Type 039/G/G1 (SSK)

Country of Origin: China

Operators: China

Active: 13

Name (Pennant Number): (39) 320, (39G) 314, 321, 322, 323, 324, (39G1) 315, 316, 318, 327

SPECIFICATION

Displacement, tons: 1,700 surfaced, 2,250 submerged.

Length, feet (meters): 245'9" (74.9) oa.

Beam, feet (meters): 27'7" (8.4) oa.

Draught, feet (meters): 23'11" (7.3).

Speed, knots: 15 surfaced; 22 submerged.

Complement: 60.

ARMAMENT

Missiles: From 21-in/533mm tubes (up to 16) ASCM – YJ-82/C-801Q Sardine.

Torpedoes: 6 x 21-in/533mm with (16-20) Yu-1, Yu-3, or Yu-4 torpedoes.

Mines: up to 36 instead of torpedoes.

Decoys: SRW209/Type 921A ESM.

SENSORS

Sonars: (active/passive) TM-2233 bow-mounted, (passive) H/SQG-04 hull-mounted, TSM-2255 flank array

RECOGNITION FEATURES

- Blunt, rounded bow, relatively low-profile hull in tear-drop shape.
- Elongated fin sited forward of midships with navigation windows, stepped, rising aft.
- 2 pairs of small driving planes on fin; one pair at leading edge, low-height and the second pair on aft edge at higher height.
- Rudder, with flat top, angled aft.

Note: Equipped with AIP engine system.

Note: (039G) does not have a step in its fin (conning tower).

Xia

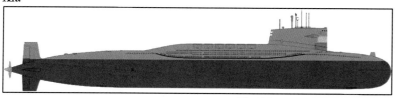

Class: Xia Type 092 (SSBN)

Country of Origin: China	
Operators: China	

Active: 1

Name (Pennant Number): CHANGZHENG 6 (406)

SPECIFICATION

Displacement, tons: 8,000 submerged.

Length, feet (meters): 393'8" (120) oa.

Beam, feet (meters): 32'10" (10) oa.

Draft, feet (meters): 26'3" (8).

Range, miles: unlimited.

Speed, knots: 22 submerged.

Complement: 100.

ARMAMENT

Missiles: 12 x SLBM - JL-1/CSS-N-3, upgraded to JL-2/CSS-NX-14.

Torpedoes: 6 x 21-in/533mm for (12) Yu-3, Yu-4 torpedoes.

RECOGNITION FEATURES

- Blunt, rounded, low bow increases in profile fin, located forward midships, and VLS cells sited amidships, in teardrop-shaped hull.
- Elongated, low profile fin sited forward of midships.
- Large driving planes on fin at leading edge, mid-height.
- Raised flat-topped missile casing aft of the fin with forward end molded round aft edge of fin. Missile casing runs flat about half the distance to the stern where it tapers away.
- Rudder, with flat top, angled aft tail.

Decoys: Type 921A ESM.

SENSORS

Surface search: MRK-50/Snoop Tray.

Sonars: (active/passive) sonar bow-mounted, (passive) SQG-04 hull-mounted, Type H/SQ2-262B hull-mounted, DUUX-5.

Yuan

Class: Yuan Type 039A/B (SSK)

Country of Origin: China	
Operators: China	
Active: 17	
Planned: 20	

Name (Pennant Number): (39A) 330, 331, 332, 333, (039B) 334, 335, 336, 337, 338, 339, 340, 341, 342, 343, 344, 345, 346, 347, (039C) ---, ---

SPECIFICATION

Displacement, tons: 2,725 surfaced, 3,600 submerged.

Length, feet (meters): 254'7" (77.6) oa.

Beam, feet (meters): 27'7" (8.4) oa.

Draft, feet (meters): 30' (6.7).

Speed, knots: 20 submerged.

Complement: 36.

ARMAMENT

Missiles: From 21-in/533mm tubes A/S – CY-1; ASCM – YJ-18, YJ-82/C-801 Sardine.

Torpedoes: 6 x 21-in/533mm with Yu-3, Yu-4, or Yu-6 torpedoes.

Decoys: Type 921A ESM.

SENSORS

Surface search: MRK-50/Snoop Tray.

Sonars: (active/passive) sonar bow-mounted, (passive) SQG-04 hull-mounted, (39B) (passive) H/SQG-207/Type 039B/C flank sonar array.

RECOGNITION FEATURES

- Blunt, rounded bow, relatively high profile hull in tear-drop shape.
- Cylindrical fin sited forward of midships with navigation windows.
- Large driving planes on fin at leading edge, mid-height.
- Rudder, with flat top, angled aft.

Note: Equipped with AIP engine system.

Note: Primary visual difference between 39A and 39B is 39B's flank array sonar attached to the lower portion of the hull.

Akula

Class: Akula Project 971 Shchuka-B (SSN)

Country of Origin: Soviet Union

Operators: Russia

Active: 8

Name (Pennant Number): MAGADAN (K 331), VEPR (K 157), VOLK (K 461), KUZBASS (K 419), LEOPARD (K 328), TIGR (K 154), SAMARA (K-295), NERPA (K 267).

SPECIFICATION

Displacement, tons: 7,500 surfaced, 9,100 submerged.

Length, feet (meters): 361'11" (110.3) oa.

Beam, feet (meters): 40'6" (15.4) oa.

Draught, feet (meters): 32'6" (9.9).

Speed, knots: 11 surfaced; 33 submerged.

Complement: 73 (33 Officers, 40 Enlisted)

ARMAMENT

Missiles: A/S – Novator SS-N-15 Starfish from 533 mm tubes, SS-N-16 Stallion from 650mm tubes with 200 kT nuclear warhead or Type 40 torpedoes; SAM – SA-N5/8 Strela portable launcher; SLCM – RKV-500 Granat/SS-N-21 Sampson from 533mm tubes.

Ilya Kurganov Photo (CC BY-SA 3.0)

RECOGNITION FEATURES

- Blunt-nosed bow, high-profile flat-topped hull with after midships gradual slope to rudder at stern.
- Long, rounded sail with near-vertical forward edge and sloped aft edge.
- Retractable diving planes built into hull at mid-heigh, aft of bow.
- Bulbous pod fitted atop rudder houses towed array sonar dispenser.

Note: Shares hull design with Sierra class. Distinguished by different sail.

Torpedoes: 4 x 21-in/533 mm and 4 x 25.6-in/650 mm tubes.

Decoys: 6 x REPS-324 launchers to hold MG-74 Korund-2, MG-104 Brosok, MG-114 Berill torpedo decoy.

SENSORS

Surface search: Snoop Pair or Snoop Half with back-to-back aerials on same mast as ESM.

Sonars: MGK-503 Skat/Shark Gill hull-mounted, MG-519 Mouse Roar hull-mounted; Skat 3 towed array.

Borei

Class: Dolgorukiy Project 955 Borei (SSBN)

Country of Origin: Soviet Union

Operators: Russia

Active: 6 + 1 in sea trials

Building: 3

Name (Pennant Number): ST PETERSBURG (K 535), ALEXANDER NEVSKY (K 550), VLADIMIR MONOMAKH (K 551), KNYAZ VLADIMIR (K 549), KNYAZ OLEG (552), GENERALISIMUS SUVOROV (553), IMPERATOR ALEXANDER III (554), KNYAZ POZHARSKIY (---), DMITRY DONSKOY (---), KNYAZ POTEMKIN (---).

RECOGNITION FEATURES

- Blunt, rounded bow.
- Slender fin sited forward of midships.
- Slightly-raised, gradually curved missile casing aft of the fin which runs straight from fin to stern, gradually tapering to the tail.
- Rudder, with curved, sloping forward edge and sloping aft edge visible aft.

Note: No diving planes on sail (conning tower)

SPECIFICATION

Displacement, tons: 13,000 surfaced, 24,000 submerged.

Length, feet (meters): 524'11" (160) oa.

Beam, feet (meters): 39'4" (12) oa.

Draft, feet (meters): 26'3" (8).

Speed, knots: 15 surfaced; 20 submerged.

Ranges, miles: Unlimited.

Complement: 102 (55 Officers, 47 Enlisted)

ARMAMENT

Missiles: (16) D-30 Bulava-M missile complex for SLBM - 3M30 RSM-56 Bulava-M/SS-NX-30 SLBM with 6-10 x 100-150 kT MIRV; SAM – (8) 9M38 Igla/9M39/SA-18 Grouse.

Torpedoes: 4 x 21-in/533mm bow torpedo tubes for SAET-60M, UGT, RPK-6 Vodopad-PL 83R/84R.

Decoys: Molniya-M; 6 x REPS-324 Shlagbaum tubes for MG-104 Brosok, MG-114 Berill, Lasta torpedo decoys.

SENSORS

Surface search: R-43 RLKS/R-43M-955A, M

Sonars: (active/passive) GK-600B Irtysh-Amfora, (navigation) Simphoniya-3.1.

Delta III/IV

Class: Delta III/IV Project 667 BDR Kalmar / 667 BDRM Delfin (SSBN)

Country of Origin: Soviet Union

Operators: Russia

Active: 7; (III) 1, (IV) 6

Name (Pennant Number): (III) ORENBURG (K 129); (IV) VERKHOTURYE (K 51), PODMOSKOVYE (K 64), TULA (K 114), BRYANSK (K 117), KARELIA (K 18), NOVOMOSKOVSK (K 407).

SPECIFICATION

Displacement, tons: 10,800 surfaced, 13,500 submerged.

Length, feet (meters): 544'7" (166) oa.

Beam, feet (meters): 39'5" (12) oa.

Draft, feet (meters): 28'6" (8.7).

Speed, knots: 14 surfaced; 24 submerged

Complement: 130 (40 Officers, 90 Enlisted)

ARMAMENT

Missiles: A/S – Novator SS-N-15 Starfish fired from 533 mm tubes or Type 40 torpedo; SLBM – RSM 5 Makeyev/SS-N-23 Skiff with 4-10 MIed 100 kT nuclear warheads.

Torpedoes: 4 x 21-in/533 mm tubes.

SENSORS

Surface search: MRP-25 Snoop Tray.

Navigation: Shlyuz.

Sonars: MGK-503 Skat/Shark Gill hull-mounted, MG-519 Mouse Roar hull-mounted; Pelamida towed array.

RECOGNITION FEATURES

- Blunt, rounded bow.
- Raised, flat-topped "turtleback" aft of sail houses VLS tubes. Runs after midships before gradual, aft-angled slope tapers hull to rudder.
- Sail mounted forward of midships, with large driving planes fitted to sail forward, mid-height.
- Rudder, with sloping forward edge visible aft.

Kilo

Konflikty.pl Photo

Class: Kilo Project 877 Paltus/636 Varshavyanka (SSK)

Country of Origin: Soviet Union	
Operators: China, Russia	

Active: 12 China (Pr. 877) 10 (Pr. 636) 2; 21 Russia (Pr. 877) (Pr. 636) 11

Building: 3

Name (Pennant Number): (China) (Pr. 877) YUAN ZHENG 64 HAO (364), YUAN ZHENG 65 HAO (365), (Pr. 636) YUAN ZHENG 66 HAO (366), YUAN ZHENG 67 HAO (367), YUAN ZHENG 67 HAO (367), YUAN ZHENG 68 HAO (368), YUAN ZHENG 69 HAO (369), YUAN ZHENG 70 HAO (370), YUAN ZHENG 71 HAO (371), YUAN ZHENG 72 HAO (372), YUAN ZHENG 73 HAO (373), YUAN ZHENG 74 HAO (374), YUAN ZHENG 75 HAO (375); (Russia) (Pr. 877) KALUGA (B 800), DMITROV (B 806), NURLAT (B 394), UST-KAMCHATSK (B 464), VLADIKAVKAZ (B 459), ALROSA (B 871), MAGNITOGORSK (B 471), UST-BOLSHERETSK (B 494), KOMSOMOLSK-ON-AMUR (B 187), LIPETSK (B 177),(Pr. 636) NOVOROSSIYSK (B 261), ROSTOV-ON-DON (B 237), STARY ORYOL (B 262), KRASNODAR (B 265), VELIKIY NOVGOROD (B 268), KOLPINO (B 271), PETROPAVLOVSK-KAMCHATSKY (B 274), VOLKHOV (B 603), MAGADAN (B 602), UFA (B 588), MOZHAYSK (608), YAKUTSK (---), PETROZAVODSK (---), MARIUPOL (---).

SPECIFICATION

Displacement, tons: 2,325 surfaced, 3,075 submerged.

Length, feet (meters): 243'9" (74.3) oa.

Beam, feet (meters): 32'6" (9.9) oa.

Draft, feet (meters): 21'8" (6.6).

Speed, knots: 10 surfaced; 17 submerged.

Ranges, miles: 7,500 at 7 kts with snorkel, 400 at 3 kts submerged.

Complement: 60 (16 Officers, 44 Enlisted)

RECOGNITION FEATURES

- Blunt, rounded bow with gradual slope in hull running from bow to stern.
- Long fin with 2 navigation windows, flat-top and vertical forward and aft edges.
- Retractable diving planes mounted high in hull, aft of bow.
- Stern diving planes not visible.

ARMAMENT

Missiles: SAM – 9M313/SA-N-5/8 Gremlin; ASCM – 3M-54E1 Novator Alfa Klub/SS-N-27.

Mines: 24 x DM-1.

Torpedoes: 6 x 21-in/533 mm tubes with TEST 71ME and 53-65. torpedoes.

Decoys: MG-74 Korund-2 decoys.

SENSORS

Surface search: MRK-50 Kaskad/Snoop Tray 2.

Navigation: SRO-2/Khrom IFF.

Sonars: MGK-400 Rubikon/Shark Teeth/Shark Fin hull-mounted, MG-512 Vint, MG-519 Arfa/Mouse Roar mine detection hull-mounted, MG-53 noise detection sonar, MG-553 Shkert.

Lada

Class: Lada Project 677/E Amur (SSN)

Country of Origin: Russia

Operators: Russia

Active: 2

Building: 3

Name (Pennant Number): (Pr. 667) KRONSHTADT (B 586), (Pr. 677E) VELIKIYE LUKI (B 587), VOLOGDA (---), YAROSLAVL (---), --- (---).

SPECIFICATION

Displacement, tons: (677) 1,450 surfaced, 2,100 submerged, (677E) 1,765 surfaced, 2,650 submerged.

Length, feet (meters): (677) 190'3" (58), (677E) 219'2" (66.8) oa.

Beam, feet (meters): (677) 23'7" (7.2), (677E) 23'4" (7.1) oa.

Draft, feet (meters): 15'9" (4.8).

Speed, knots: 17 surfaced; 21 kts submerged.

Range, miles: 4,0000 at 7 kts under schnorkel.

Complement: (677) 34, (677E) 35.

ARMAMENT

Missiles: (677E) SAM - 6 x 1 (6) Igla-1M/SA-18 Grouse.

Torpedoes: 6 x 21-in/533mm bow tubes for 16 53-56B, SET-53M torpedoes.

Mines: 22 DM-1 instead of torpedoes.

SENSORS

Surface search: KRM-66 Kodak integrated radar system.

Sonars: Lira hull-mounted.

RECOGNITION FEATURES

- Blunt, rounded bow.
- Teardrop shaped hull, relatively high profile in the water.
- Long fin with vertical leading and aft edges, flat top, navigation windows, and diving planes fitted forward and mid-height.
- Rudder visible, but hull dips below waterline in profile.

Note: Equipped with an AIP system.

Oscar II

US Navy Photo

Class: Oscar II Project 949A Antei (SSGN)

Country of Origin: Soviet Union

Operators: Russia

Active: 7

Name (Pennant Number): BELGOROD (BS 329), CHELYABINSK (K 442), IRKUTSK (K 132), OMSK (K 186), ORYEL (K 266), SMOLENSK (K 410), TOMSK (K 150), TVER (K 456).

SPECIFICATION

Displacement, tons: 13,900 surfaced, 18,300 submerged.

Length, feet (meters): 505'3" (154) oa.

Beam, feet (meters): 59'8" (18.2) oa.

Draft, feet (meters): 29'6" (9).

Speed, knots: 15 surfaced; 33 submerged.

Complement: 109 (44 Officers, 65 Enlisted).

ARMAMENT

Missiles: A/S – Novator/SS-N-15 Starfish from 533mm tubes, Novator/SS-N-16 Stallion from 650mm tubes with payload Type 45 Veder torpedo or Vodopad 200 kT nuclear warhead; SSM – 24 x Chelomey Granit/SS-N-19 Shipwreck with 750 kg HE or 500 kT nuclear warhead.

Torpedoes: 4 x 21-in/533 mm tubes, 4 x 25.6-in/650mm tubes with Type 53, Type 65 torpedoes.

RECOGNITION FEATURES

- Blunt, rounded bow.
- Wide hull with rounded top and rounded bulge aft of bow, forward sail.
- Thin sail with rounded, tapered top, vertical forward and aft edges.
- Sail includes navigational windows at top, forward edge.
- VLS cells fitted in 2 rows of 12 tubes on port and starboard side of sail.
- Retractable diving planes mounted high in hull, aft of bow.
- Vertical rudder visible at stern.

SENSORS

Surface search: Albatros/Snoop Pair or Snoop Half.

Sonars: Shark Gill (Skat MGK-503/Shark Gill hull-mounted, Shark Rib flank array, MG-519/Mouse Roar hull-mounted; Pelamida towed array.

Severodvinsk

Class: Severodvinsk Project 885M Yasen (SSN)

Country of Origin: Soviet Union

Operators: Russia

Active: 3 + 1 in sea trials

Building: 5

Name (Pennant Number): SEVERODVINSK (840), KAZAN (K-830), ARKHANGELSK (K-564), KRASNOYARSK (K-571), NOVOSIBIRSK (K-573), PERM (---), ULYANOVSK (---), VORONEZH (---), VLADIVOSTOK (---).

SPECIFICATION

Displacement, tons: 9,500 surfaced, 11,800 submerged.

Length, feet (meters): 456'8" (139.2) oa.

Beam, feet (meters): 42'8" (13) oa.

Draught, feet (meters): 30'10" (9.4).

Speed, knots: 16 surfaced; 28 submerged.

Range, miles: unlimited.

Complement: 85 (32 Officers, 53 Enlisted).

ARMAMENT

Missiles: 8 x 4 (32) launchers including ASCM – 3K55 Oniks/SS-N-26 Strobile, 3M14K Kalibr/SS-N-27 Sizzler; for launch by torpedo tube instead of torpedoes (30) (ASCM) 3K10

Ministry of Defense of Russia Photo

RECOGNITION FEATURES

- Low, blunt bow.
- Large diameter, bulbous hull with high profile.
- Rounded top to casing.
- Rounded fin sited forward of midships with slightly sloping leading edge and long sloping aft edge.
- Large, aft-protruding tail on rudder.

Note: Severodvinsk-class does not have diving planes.

Granat/SS-N-21 Sampson, 3K22 Zircon/SS-N-33.

Torpedoes: 10 x 21-in/533mm tubes including (30) Type 53 UGST torpedoes and missiles (above).

SENSORS

Surface search: MRKP-43.

Navigation: Medveditsa-M complex.

Sonars: MGK-600 Irtysh-Amfora-Yasen sonar complex, Ayaks sonar.

Sierra I/II

Class: Sierra I/II Project 945 Barracuda /045A Kondor (SSN)

Country of Origin: Soviet Union	
Operators: Russia	

Active: 4

Name (Pennant Number): (945) KARP (K 239), TULA (K 276); (945A) NIZNHIY NOVGOROD (K 534), PSKOV (K336).

SPECIFICATION

Displacement, tons: (945) 6,170 surfaced, 8,200 submerged; (945A) 6,466 surfaced, 8,500 submerged.

Length, feet (meters): (945) 351'8" (107.2); (945A) 362'10" (110.6) oa.

Beam, feet (meters): 40'4" (12.3) oa.

Draft, feet (meters): (945) 31'6" (9.6); (945A) 31'2" (9.5).

Speed, knots: (945) 12 surfaced; 35 submerged; (945A) 14 surfaced, 33 submerged.

Complement: (945) 67 (31 Officers, 33 Enlisted); (945A) 71 (33 Officers, 38 Enlisted).

ARMAMENT

Missiles: instead of torpedoes, can include ASCM - RKP-55 Granat/SS-N-21 Sampson; A/S – RPK,RPK-7/SS-N_16 Vodoad/Veter/Stallion ASROC; SAM - (1) Strela.

Torpedoes: 4 x 21-in/533 mm, 4 x 25.6-in/650 mm tubes with (40) SAET-60M, Type 65-76, Type 53-65K torpedoes.

Decoys: MG-74 Korund torpedo decoys.

RECOGNITION FEATURES

- Blunt-nosed bow, high-profile flat-topped hull with after midships gradual slope to rudder at stern.
- Long, wide sail fitted midships with navigation windows and small diving planes fitted forward and high-height.
- Retractable diving planes built into hull at mid-height, aft of bow.
- Bulbous pod fitted atop rudder houses towed array sonar dispenser.

Note: Shares hull design with Akula class. Distinguished by different sail.

SENSORS

Surface search: MRKP-58 Radian/Snoop Pair, (945) MRP-21 (945A) MRP-23.

Sonars: (active-passive) MG-500 Skat/Shark Gill hull-mounted, with towed array.

Uniform

US Navy Photo

Class: Uniform Project 1910 Kashalot (SSAN)

Country of Origin: Soviet Union

Operators: Russia

Active: 2

Name (Pennant Number): AS-13, AS-15.

SPECIFICATION

Displacement, tons: 1,390 surfaced, 1,580 submerged.

Length, feet (meters): 226'5" (69) oa.

Beam, feet (meters): 23' (7) oa.

Draft, feet (meters): 17'1" (5.2).

Speed, knots: 10 surfaced; 30 submerged.

Complement: 36.

SENSORS

Surface search: SS-N-3/12 Burya/Snoop Slab.

Sonars: Gnays-5MK sonar complex.

RECOGNITION FEATURES

- Blunt, rounded bow with distinctive cylindrical hull.
- Flat top of hull runs from bow almost to rudder, with sloped aft edge.
- Rudder profile is sloped aft, ending in vertical end edge.
- Bridge mounted forward of midships, with aft-angled aft end.
- Distinctive lack of sail on bridge.
- Mast mounted after bridge, forward of midships.

Note: Single hull is constructed of titanium.

125

Victor III

Class: Victor III Project 671RTMK Shchuka (SSN)

Country of Origin: Soviet Union

Operators: Russia

Active: 2

Name (Pennant Number): OBNINSK (B 138), TAMBOV (B 448).

SPECIFICATION

Displacement, tons: 4,850 surfaced, 6,300 submerged.

Length, feet (meters): 351 (107) oa.

Beam, feet (meters): 34'9" (10.6) oa.

Draft, feet (meters): 24'3" (7.4).

Speed, knots: 10 surfaced; 30 submerged.

Complement: 92 (23 Officers, 69 Enlisted)

ARMAMENT

Missiles: A/S – Novator SS-N-15 Starfish from 533mm tubes with 200 kT Vodopad nuclear warhead or Veder Type 40 torpedo; SAM – SA-N-8 Gremlin when surfaced; SLCM – Granat/SS-N-21 Sampson from 533mm tubes.

Torpedoes: 4 x 21-in/533mm tubes , 2 x 25.6-in/650mm tubes.

RECOGNITION FEATURES

- Rounded, blunt bow with teardrop-shaped hull sloping aft from bow to vertical rudder at stern.
- Retractable, hull-mounted diving planes.
- Retractable diving planes mounted high in hull, aft of bow.
- Streamlined pod mounted atop vertical rudder at stern, houses towed sonar array dispenser.

Mines: Up to 36 RM-2G Goletc mines instead of torpedoes.

Decoys: MG-74 Korund-2 torpedo decoy.

SENSORS

Surface search: MRP-25/Snoop Tray.

Sonars: MGK-503 Skat/Shark Gill hull-mounted, Shark Rib flank array, MG-519/Mouse Roar hull-mounted; Skat 3 towed array.

Code	Reporting Title	Description
AA	Auxiliary type ship, general	General designator for all naval auxiliary type ships
AH	Hospital ship	Ship 40 m or more providing hospital services
AP	Personnel transport	Ship of 120 m or more, transporting troops and supplies
CA	Cruiser, gun	Cruiser with 6 in guns or larger as primary armament and no missiles
CC	Cruiser, general	Surface combatant ships 150 m or longer
CG	Cruisers, guided missile	Cruiser with guided missiles as primary armament
CGH	Cruiser, guided missile, helicopter	Guided missile cruiser with helicopter operational capability
CGN	Cruiser, guided missile, nuclear	Guided missile cruiser with nuclear propulsion
CV	Aircraft carrier	Designator for aircraft carriers and multi-role aircraft carriers
CVH	Aircraft carrier, VSTOL/helicopter	Carrier without arrest gear/catapult, operating VSTOL and/or helicopters and not an amphibious or mine warfare vessel
CVN	Aircraft carrier, nuclear	Carrier with nuclear propulsion
DD	Destroyer, general	General designator for surface combatants 95-140 m long
DDG	Destroyer, guided missile	Destroyer equipped with surface-to-air guided missiles
FF	Frigate/corvette general	General designator for surface combatants 75-150 m long. Lighter armament than destroyers.
FFG	Frigate, guided missile	Frigate equipped with surface-to-air guided missiles.
FS	Corvette	Escort vessel 60-100 m long.
FSG	Corvette, guided missile	Corvette equipped with surface-to-air guided missiles.
LCC	Amphibious command ship	Command ship for amphibious task forces and landing operations.
LCAC	Landing craft, air cushion	Landing craft reliant on air cushion for buoyancy and landing
LCM	Landing craft, mechanized	Landing craft 15-25m, capable of carrying 1 tank or 50-200 troops
LCP	Landing craft, personnel	Landing craft 7.5-30m suitable only for personnel
LCU	Landing craft, utility	All-purpose landing craft 25-55m with landing ramp, able to carry 2-3 tanks or 300-450 troops.
LHA	Amphibious general assault ship	Large all-purpose ships for landing assault forces by helicopter
LHD	Amphibious assault ship, multipurpose	Amphibious assault ships with internal storage and also a flooded ramp able to land forces by own landing craft
LL	Amphibious vessel, general	General designator for amphibious vessels
LPA	Amphibious transport, personnel	Ships able to carry 1300-1500 troops and land them with own craft
LPD	Amphibious transport, dock	Ships capable of carrying 1000 troops, up to 9 LCMs, and have a helicopter platform.
LPH	Amphibious assault ship	Helicopter carrier for landing up to 1800 troops with own aircraft
LSD	Landing ship, dock	A tank and vehicle carrier capable of carrying 150-400 troops
LSM	Landing ship, medium	Ships 45-85 m long capable of beaching to land troops & tanks.
LST	Landing ship, tank	Ships 85-160 m long carrying troops, vehicles, and tanks for amphibious assault landings
LVTP	Landing vehicle, tracked, personnel	Tracked amphibious vehicle capable of carrying troops
MM	Mine warfare vessels, general	General designator for mine warfare vessels
MCM	Mine countermeasures vessel	Minehunter with mechanical and influence sweep capability
MH	Minehunter, general	Fitted with equipment to hunt mines, 25-60 m long with enhanced minehunting capability. May carry sweep gear and divers.
MHS	Minehunter & sweeper, general	Ships designed to sweep or lay mines
MLC	Minelayer, coastal	Ships designed to lay mines in coastal zones, 40-60 m long.
MSC	Minesweeper, coastal	Ships designed to sweep mines in coastal zones, 40-60 m long
MSO	Minesweeper, ocean	Ships designed to sweep mines oceanic zones, 46 m or longer.
OPV	Offshore patrol vessel	Ships designated to conduct patrols in open ocean.
PC(F)	Patrol craft, general fast	General designator for patrol vessels
PG	Patrol ship, general	Ships 45-85 m long, not designed for open ocean operations, and have at least 3 in/76 mm gun armament
PG (G)	Patrol ship, general (guided missile)	Patrol ships equipped with guided missiles.
PHM	Patrol combatant, guided missile	High speed (hydrofoil) craft with surface-surface guided missiles
PT(H)	Patrol/torpedo boat (hydrofoil)	High speed (35 kts) craft 20-30 m long with anti-surface torpedoes
SS	Submarine, general	General designator for submarines
SSBN	Submarine, ballistic missile, nuclear	Nuclear Submarines with nuclear warhead ballistic missiles.
SSGN	Submarine, guided missile, nuclear	Nuclear Submarines, equipped with guided missiles
SSK	Submarine, patrol	Non-nuclear submarines with anti-surface or anti-submarine role.
SSN	Submarine, attack, nuclear	Nuclear submarines with anti-surface or anti-submarine role.

ENSIGNS & JACKS

Ensign – A flag which identifies the nationality of a maritime vessel. Usually flown from the stern.

Jack – A flag flown from a ship's jackstaff.

Naval Jack of China

Union Jack

Ensign of America

Ensign of Russia

Ensign of Iran

Naval Jack of America

Naval Ensign of Russia

Naval Jack of Iran

First Naval Jack of America

Naval Jack of Russia

Ensign of North Korea

Coast Guard Ensign of America

Border Guard Ensign of Russia

Naval Jack of North Korea

Ensign of China

Ensign of France

Ensign of Japan

Naval Ensign of China

Ensign of Great Britain

Naval Jack of Japan

WEAPON SYSTEMS

Aircraft – An integral component of naval warfare since the Second World War, both manned and unmanned fixed-wing and rotary aircraft provide reconnaissance, strike, and transportation capabilities in the maritime domain.

Decoys – Countermeasures to defeat enemy sensors and preempt guided missiles attacks.

Directed Energy – Lasers and microwave emitters used either defensively to defeat incoming threats, or offensively to inflict damage on enemy targets at sea, ashore, or in the air.

Electronic – Various electronic warfare capabilities designed to disrupt (jam) enemy use of the electro-magnetic spectrum for communication and sensing, to include radars and communications equipment, or to subvert (spoof) equipment readings to misinform and misdirect the enemy.

Guns – Traditional naval weapons designed to launch munitions at enemy targets to inflict kinetic damage on enemy targets. Sized according to caliber, the internal diameter of a gun barrel.

Mines – Area denial weapons consisting of explosives and sensors attached (moored) to a specific location. Can be found on the surface, undersea, or anchored directly to the seabed.

Missiles – The predominant form of naval weaponry, consists of a wide-range of airborne, self-propelled projectiles, usually equipped with guidance systems and categorized by their intended target; air-to-air, air-to-surface, surface-to-air, surface-to-surface, and anti-satellite. Comprised of four system components: a guidance system, flight system, engine, and a warhead.

Radars – Quintessential sensors for modern naval warfare. Radio Detection and Ranging (RADAR) is a detection system that uses radio waves to determine the range, angle, and velocity of objects. Comprised of a transmitter producing electromagnetic waves in the radio or microwaves domain, a transmitting antenna, a receiving antenna (can be the same), and a receiver and processor to assess the detected object. Categorized as long-range air search, air search, navigation, fire control, surface search, and undersea (sonars).

Torpedoes – the predominant weapon for undersea warfare, torpedoes are self-propelled underwater sea mines usually equipped with guidance systems. Modern torpedoes are categorized by their relative weight (light, medium, heavy) and by guidance system as straight-running, autonomous homing-guided, and wire-guided.

ACRONYMS

AAW	Anti-Air Warfare
AESA	Active Electronic Scanned Array
AEW	Airborne Early Warning
AIP	Air Independent Propulsion
AGM	Attack Guided Missile
AMDR	Air and Missile Defense Radar
AN	Array, Navy (sensor designation)
AN/SPY	Array, Navy/Search Protect Yellow
A/S, ASW	Anti-Submarine, Anti-Submarine Warfare
ASM	Air-To-Surface Missile
ASROC	Anti-Submarine Rocket-Assisted Torpedo
AV	Attack, VSTOL
BMD	Ballistic Missile Defense
BTR	Wheeled Infantry Fighting Vehicle
Cal./Caliber	Gun barrel diameter
CADS	Close-in Air Defense System
CATOBAR	Catapult Assisted Take Off But Arrested Recovery
CIWS	Close-In Weapon System
DBR	Dual Band Radar
Displacement	Weight of water displaced by a ship's hull when floating.
EA	Electronic Warfare/Attack aircraft
EASR	Enterprise Air Surveillance Radar
ECM	Electronic Countermeasures
EMALS	Electromagnetic Aircraft Launch System
EO/IR	Electro-Optical Infrared
ERAM	Extended Range Active Missile
ESB	Expeditionary Mobile Base
ESM	Electronic Support Measures
ESSM	Evolved Sea Sparrow Missile
EW	Electronic Warfare
F/A	Fighter / Attack aircraft
FAC	Fast Attack Craft
FIM	Man-portable air-defense missile
GMLS	Guided Missile Launch System
GPS	Global Positioning System
IFF	Identification Friend/Foe
ICMS	Integrated Combat Management System
in	Inch(es)
ITAS	Integrated Target Acquisition System
Ka	Kamov
kts	Knots - speed of 1 nautical mile per hour.
LAB	Large Aperture Bow
LAMPS	Light Airborne Multipurpose System
LCCA	Low-Cost Conformal Array
MAD	Magnetic Anomaly Detector
MBT	Main Battle Tank
MCM	Mine Counter Measures
MDG	Magnetometer Degaussing System
MFCS	Missile Fire Control System
MFTA	Multifunction Towed Array
MG	Machine Gun
MH	Multi-mission Helicopter
MIDAS	Mine and Ice Avoidance System
Mk	Mark (version or type)
MOD	Modified/modification
MQ	Multi-mission Unmanned Aircraft
MRLS	Multiple Rocket Launch System

MV	Multi-mission VSTOL aircraft
nm	Nautical Mile
NSM	Navy Strike Missile
NSSM	NATO Sea Sparrow Missile
oa	Overall length between extremities
OTH	Over The Horizon (radar)
RAM	Rolling Airframe Missile
RBU	Antisubmarine Rocket
RGM	Radar Guided Missile
RIM	Rocket Intercept Missile
RGM	Submarine-Launched Guided Missile
RUM	Submarine-Launched Underwater Missile
RO-RO	Roll-On, Roll-Off
RWR	Radio Warning Receiver
SAM	Surface-to-Air Missile
SEWIP	Surface Electronic Warfare Improvement Program
SLBM	Submarine-Launched Ballistic Missile
SLCM	Submarine-Launched Cruise Missile
SRBOC	Super Rapid Blooming Offboard Chaff
SSM	Surface-to-Surface Missile
SWFTS	Submarine Warfare Federated Tactical System
TACAN	Tactical Air Navigation System
TACTASS	Tactical Towed-Acoustic Sensor System
TAS	Target Acquisition System
TASM	Tomahawk Anti-Ship Missile
TLAM-N	Tomahawk Land Attack Missile - Nuclear
UGM	Underwater Guided Missile
USV	Unmanned Surface Vessel
VDS	Variable Depth Sonar
VL	Vertical Launch
VLS	Vertical Launch System
VSTOL	Vertical or Short Takeoff and Landing
wl	Water Line. Measurement of length between extremities at the water line.
WSN	Wireless and Satellite Network

Made in the USA
Columbia, SC
17 August 2024

9bb88440-2276-4922-b559-6bcf41d35f90R01